Bookkeeping Workbook For Dummies®

CU00956212

Key Guiding Principles for Controlling Your Business Cash

- Separate cash handlers (whether by cash, credit, or checks). Be sure the person who records a transaction is not the same as the person who accepts the cash.
- Separate authorization responsibilities. Be sure the person who authorizes a payment is not the same person as the one who signs the check or disperses the cash.
- Separate the duties of your bookkeeping function to be sure there is a good system of checks and balances. Make sure you don't put too much trust in one person.
- Separate operational responsibility (actual day-to-day transactions) from record-keeping responsibility (the one who enters the transactions in the books).

Tracking Cash — Things You Must Do after You Get the Money

- Record transactions in your books.
- Track individual customer accounts.
- Record any discounts that were offered.
- Track any returns or allowances that were given to customers.
- Collect from customers to whom you sell on credit.
- Monitor customer accounts to be sure they pay on time.
- Write off accounts from customers who just won't pay.

Credits and Debits of Double-Entry Bookkeeping

All transactions are entered in the books twice, once as a debit and once as a credit. This chart shows you how debits and credits impact your accounts:

Account Type	Debits	Credits
Assets	Increase	Decrease
Liabilities	Decrease	Increase
Income	Decrease	Increase
Expenses	Increase	Decrease

Bookkeeping Workbook For Dummies®

Cheat Sheet

Key Parts of a Bookkeeping System

- **Chart of Accounts:** Serves as a road map to a business's financial transactions. Lists all accounts in the books.
- **Journals:** Place in the books where transactions are first entered.
- **General Ledger:** A book that summarizes all a business's account transactions.

Key Steps in Keeping the Books

- **Transactions:** A purchase or sale of an item starts the process of bookkeeping.
- **Journal entries:** Transactions are first entered into the books through journals.
- **Posting:** Journal entries are posted to the General Ledger.
- **Trial balance:** Accounts in the General Ledger are tested to see whether they are in balance.
- **Worksheet:** Adjustments that are needed to accounts after a trial balance are entered on a worksheet.
- **Adjusting journal entries:** Adjustments from the worksheet are posted to affected accounts in the General Ledger.
- **Financial statements:** The Balance Sheet and Income Statement are then prepared using the corrected account balances.
- **Closing:** Books are closed for the Revenue and Expense accounts, and the entire cycle is started again with zero balances in the Revenue and Expense accounts.

Ways to Value Your Inventory

- **LIFO (Last In, First Out):** Assumes last (most recent) item put on the shelf is the first product sold.
- **FIFO (First In, First Out):** Assumes first (oldest) item put on the shelf is the first one sold.
- **Averaging:** You don't need to worry about what item came in first or last. Average the cost of inventory when calculating inventory value.
- **Specific identification:** Track how much you paid for each individual item to determine inventory value.

For Dummies: Bestselling Book Series for Beginners

Bookkeeping Workbook

FOR

DUMMIES®

Bookkeeping Workbook

FOR DUMMIES®

by Lita Epstein, MBA

Wiley Publishing, Inc.

Bookkeeping Workbook For Dummies®

Published by
Wiley Publishing, Inc.
111 River St.
Hoboken, NJ 07030-5774
www.wiley.com

For general information on our other products and services, please contact our Customer Care Department within the U.S. at 800-762-2974, outside the U.S. at 317-572-3993, or fax 317-572-4002.

For technical support, please visit www.wiley.com/techsupport.

Wiley also publishes its books in a variety of electronic formats. Some content that appears in print may not be available in electronic books.

ISBN: 978-0-470-16983-4

Library of Congress Control Number: 2007934458

Manufactured in the United States of America

10 9 8 7 6 5 4 3 2 1

About the Author

Lita Epstein, who earned her MBA from Emory University's Goizueta Business School, enjoys helping people develop good financial, investing and tax-planning skills.

While getting her MBA, Lita worked as a teaching assistant for the financial accounting department and ran the accounting lab. After completing her MBA, she managed finances for a small nonprofit organization and for the facilities management section of a large medical clinic.

She designs and teaches online courses on topics such as investing for retirement, getting ready for tax time and finance and investing for women. She's written over 20 books including *Reading Financial Reports For Dummies* and *Trading For Dummies*.

Lita was the content director for a financial services Web site, MostChoice.com, and managed the Web site, Investing for Women. As a Congressional press secretary, Lita gained first-hand knowledge about how to work within and around the Federal bureaucracy, which gives her great insight into how government programs work. In the past, Lita has been a daily newspaper reporter, magazine editor, and fundraiser for the international activities of former President Jimmy Carter through The Carter Center.

Dedication

To my father, Jerome Kirschbrown, who taught me the importance of accounting, bookkeeping, and watching every detail.

Author's Acknowledgments

Many people were involved in making this book a reality. First, a special thank you to Stacy Kennedy, my acquisitions editor at Wiley, who successfully championed this book through the editorial board process. Also at Wiley, a special thanks to Jennifer Connolly, my project editor, whose helpful and insightful comments, as well as her expert editing, helped make this book the best it could be. In addition, I want to thank my agent, Jessica Faust, who helps me regularly with all my book projects. And finally, last but not least, my husband, H.G. Wolpin, who puts up with all my craziness as I try to meet deadlines.

Publisher's Acknowledgments

We're proud of this book; please send us your comments through our Dummies online registration form located at www.dummies.com/register/.

Some of the people who helped bring this book to market include the following:

Acquisitions, Editorial, and Media Development

Project Editor: Jennifer Connolly

Acquisitions Editor: Stacy Kennedy

Copy Editor: Jennifer Connolly

Technical Editor: Ken Morrow

Editorial Manager: Michelle Hacker

Editorial Supervisor: Carmen Krikorian

Editorial Assistants: Erin Calligan, Joe Niesen, David Lutton, and Leann Harney

Cartoons: Rich Tennant (www.the5thwave.com)

Composition Services

Project Coordinator: Patrick Redmond

Layout and Graphics: Carl Byers, Denny Hager, Jennifer Mayberry, Melanee Prendergast, Julie Trippetti

Anniversary Logo Design: Richard Pacifico

Proofreader: Linda Quigley

Indexer: Broccoli Information Management

Publishing and Editorial for Consumer Dummies

    Diane Graves Steele, Vice President and Publisher, Consumer Dummies

    Joyce Pepple, Acquisitions Director, Consumer Dummies

    Kristin A. Cocks, Product Development Director, Consumer Dummies

    Michael Spring, Vice President and Publisher, Travel

    Kelly Regan, Editorial Director, Travel

Publishing for Technology Dummies

    Andy Cummings, Vice President and Publisher, Dummies Technology/General User

Composition Services

    Gerry Fahey, Vice President of Production Services

    Debbie Stailey, Director of Composition Services

Contents at a Glance

Table of Contents

Introduction

Bookkeepers are the keepers of the cash and the crucial caretakers of all information about the company's transactions. People both inside the business (managers, owners, and employees) and people outside the business (investors, lenders and governmental agencies) all depend on the accurate recording of financial transactions by the bookkeeper.

- ✔ Financial institutions won't loan money to a company unless they trust the financial reports that have been prepared by that company when it applies for a loan.
- ✔ Investors won't invest in a company if they don't trust its financial reporting.
- ✔ Employees need to know their job will still be there tomorrow and many employees are dependent on accurate financial reports in order to do their jobs.

If you subscribe to the idea that information is power, which I do, you'll find that the bookkeeper has a tremendous amount of power in a company. Information tracked in the books help business owners make key decisions involving sales planning, product offerings, and how to manage many other financial aspects of their business.

Whether you are an owner keeping the books yourself or you are an employee keeping the books for a small business owner, your job is critical for the smooth financial operation of the company.

Bookkeepers must be detail oriented, must enjoy working with numbers, and must be meticulous about accurately entering those numbers in a company's books. They must be good about keeping a paper trail and filing all needed backup information about the financial transactions they enter into the books.

Bookkeeping has a language and method of operation all its own. Understanding that new language and operating under the rules of bookkeeping can be foreign to anyone who's never been exposed to it before; it takes practice. In this workbook, I introduce you to the world of bookkeeping and give you opportunities to practice the key concepts.

About This Book

In this book, I take you through the continuous cycle of bookkeeping, which begins with setting up your company's books, developing a list of your company's accounts (Chart of Accounts; see Chapter 3), developing your company's General Ledger (which summarizes all the activity in a company's accounts; see Chapter 4), and developing your company's journals (which give details about all of a company's financial transactions; see Chapter 5).

Then I take you through the process of recording all your transactions — sales, purchases and other financial activity. I also talk about how to manage payroll, governmental reporting, and external financial reporting.

Finally, I show you how to start the yearly cycle all over again by closing out the necessary accounts for the current year and opening up any new ones for the next year.

However, although bookkeeping is a continuous cycle, a Dummies book is not. You don't have to follow the entire cycle or go through it in order if you don't want to. The reference style of this book allows you to skip around to the chapters you need to know more about, or you can go through all of them to practice all the skills I outline in this book.

Foolish Assumptions

While writing this book, I made some key assumptions about who you are and why you want to learn more about bookkeeping. I assume that you are

- ✔ **A business owner who wants to know how to do your own books:** You have a good understanding of business and its terminology, but have little or no knowledge of bookkeeping and accounting.
- ✔ **A person who does bookkeeping or plans to do bookkeeping for a small business and needs to know more about how to set up and keep the books:** Again I assume you have some basic knowledge of business terminology, but don't know much about bookkeeping or accounting.
- ✔ **A staff person in a small business and have just been asked to take over the bookkeeping duties for the company:** You need to know more detail about how transactions are entered into the books accurately and how to prove out the transactions that have been entered into the books.

How This Book Is Organized

I organized this workbook into six parts, which I outline in the sections below:

Part 1: Exploring Bookkeeping Basics

In Part I, I discuss the importance of bookkeeping, explain the basics about how it works, and help you get started with setting up of your books. You'll find questions and problems that will help you learn bookkeeping's unique terms and how to set up the roadmap for your books — the Chart of Accounts.

Part II: Putting It All on Paper

In Part II, I show you to how to enter your financial transactions in the books, how to post transactions to your General Ledger (the granddaddy of your bookkeeping system), how to track all the transaction details in your journals, and how to develop a good internal control system for managing your books and your company's cash. Questions and problems will give you an opportunity to practice these tasks.

Part III: Tracking Day-to-Day Business Operations with Your Books

In Part III, I show you how to track your day-to-day business operations including recording sales and purchases, as well as recording any adjustments to those sales and purchases, such as discounts and returns. In addition, I talk about the basics of setting up and managing employee payroll, as well as all the government paperwork you'll need to complete as soon as you decide to hire employees. You'll also find problems that give you an opportunity to practice how to perform these key duties of a bookkeeper.

Part IV: Getting Ready for Year's (Or Month's) End

In Part IV, I introduce you to the process of preparing your books for closing out the accounting period, whether you're closing out the books at the end of a month or the end of a year. You'll learn about the key adjustments needed to record depreciation of your assets (a process which tracks the use of your tangible assets, such as cars and buildings), which must be done before you close the books. You'll also learn about how to calculate and record your interest payments and receipts in your books. Then I'll talk about various aspects of proving out your books — checking your cash, testing the balance of your books, and making any needed adjustments or corrections. In addition, you'll find problems that will give you time to practice these tasks for preparing the books for the end of the accounting period.

Part V: Putting on Your Best Financial Face

In Part V, you explore how to report all your hard work keeping the books to others inside and outside the company. I also explore the various structures of a business and what forms must be filed with the IRS. Finally I talk about how you close out the books at year-end and get ready for the next year.

Part VI: The Part of Tens

Part VI is the hallmark of the *For Dummies* series — the Part of Tens. In it, I highlight the top ten accounts you should monitor and a top ten checklist for managing cash.

Icons Used in This Book

To make spotting certain info even easier, I use the following icons:

When I give you specific tidbits of info that can help make your efforts run smoother or more quickly, I tag them with this icon.

I use this icon when I provide you some info that I definitely don't want you to forget.

 Now, it wouldn't be any fun to work in a workbook without seeing some examples first, now would it? To make these examples easy to spot, I use this icon.

Where to Go from Here

You're now ready to enter the world of bookkeeping. You can start anywhere in the book you would like.

If you already know the bookkeeping basics, are familiar with the key terminology, and know how to set up a chart of accounts, you may want to start with Part II. If you need to learn all the basics or want to refresh your knowledge then start with Part I.

If you've got your books already set up and know the basics, you may want to start with how to enter various transactions in Part III. If your first priority is understanding how to use the financial information, then you may want to look at financial reporting options in Part V first.

Part I
Exploring Bookkeeping Basics

The 5th Wave   By Rich Tennant

"I think I'm finally getting the hang of this accounting system. It's even got a currency conversion function. Want to see how much we lost in rupees?"

In this part . . .

*B*ookkeeping can look like a foreign language to anyone who's never seen it before. In this part you'll explore the basics about how bookkeeping works. You'll also begin to relearn terms you may already think you know but have a unique meaning in the world of bookkeeping — like ledgers, journals, posting, debits and credits. Then you'll delve into how to set up the roadmap for your books — the Chart of Accounts.

Chapter 1

Deciphering the Basics

· ·

· ·

*B*ookkeepers are the accountant's eyes and ears. Few accountants actually take the time to enter the numbers into the accounting books. That job instead goes to the book-keepers. Bookkeeping, when done properly, gives a business owener an excellent gauge of how well his business is doing financially.

In this chapter, you will get an overview of a bookkeeper's work and introduction to some of the key accounting concepts.

Using Cash or Accrual Method

When setting up a business, the first major accounting decision that must be made is whether to keep the books using the cash-basis accounting method or the accrual account-ing method. If you decide to use the cash-basis accounting method, you record all transac-tions only when cash actually changes hands. Cash can include payment by cash, check credit card, electronic transfer, or any other means you pay for something you buy. If you decide to use the accrual accounting method, you record a transaction when the transaction is completed, even if cash has not yet changed hands.

For example, if your company purchases the products it plans to sell from vendors on credit and doesn't pay for them until 30 days later, you would record this transaction differently depending upon which method you choose to use. If you are using the cash-basis accounting method, you would not record the purchase in your books until you actually pay for the products with cash. If you are using the accrual method, you would record the purchase immediately. You would record the purchase in an account called Purchases and you would record the liability to the vendor in an account called Accounts Payable on the day you get the bill for the goods, which allows you to track all pending obligations to vendors.

Many small businesses run by a sole proprietor (single owner) or partnership group choose to use cash-basis accounting at first because it's easier, but as the business grows and there are many more transactions to keep track of a business usually will switch to the accrual method of accounting.

Q. You buy products for sale on June 15 on credit with the vendor and get a bill with the purchase. You don't have to pay that bill until July 1. How would you record this transaction in your books if you are using cash-basis accounting and also how would you would record it using accrual accounting?

A. For cash-basis accounting, you would not record anything in the books until you pay for the products with cash on July 1. For accrual accounting you would record the purchase on June 15 in Accounts Payable, as well as in the account where you record purchases.

1. You buy products you plan to sell paying cash on delivery on June 15. How and when would you record this transaction in your books if you are using cash-basis accounting and how would you record it using accrual accounting?

Solve It

2. You contract with a painter to paint your store front on June 15 and he completes the work on July 1 and gives you a bill for the work. You pay for the work with cash on July 5. How and when would you record this transaction in your books if you are using cash-basis accounting and how would you record it using accrual accounting?

Solve It

3. You order office supplies on credit on June 15 and receive them on June 16. You are billed for them on July 1, but don't pay for them with cash until July 15. How and when would you first record this transaction in your books if you are using cash-basis accounting and how would you record it using accrual accounting?

Solve It

4. You sell your products to a customer on store credit on June 15. You send a bill to the customer on July 1. You receive payment in cash from the customer on July 15. How and when would you first record this transaction in your books if you are using cash-basis accounting and how would you record it using accrual accounting?

Solve It

So which accounting method is better? The cash-basis accounting method does a good job of tracking the flow of cash, but it does a poor job of matching your revenues to your expenses. The accrual accounting method does a good job of matching revenues and expenses, but does a poor job of tracking the use of cash. Companies that use accrual accounting also set up a system to monitor cash flow.

The biggest difference between these two methods shows up with transactions that occur at the end of one year and the beginning of the next year. As you work through these problems you will see how differently the transactions are handled at the end of a year for each accounting method and how the way they are handled can impact the profits and expenses you show on your financial statements, as well as the taxes you may have to pay on any profits at the end of the year.

There is a big difference between cash and accrual accounting. While cash accounting is easier, it does make it more difficult to keep track of money due from customers who buy on store credit, as well as payments due to vendors, suppliers, contractors, and others for purchases and other expenses. You should never choose to use the cash-basis accounting method if:

Your business carries over inventory month-to-month and year-to-year. It is more difficult to match costs for the inventory with the profits made from the sale of that inventory using the cash-basis method.

Your business allows customers to buy on store credit. Your books will not show the revenue until the customers pay in cash. Also, you will have a more difficult time tracking how much is due from customers.

You decide to incorporate your business. Read chapter 17 for more on business types.

You have gross annual sales of more than $5 million.

If you do start keeping your books using the cash-basis accounting method, you can convert to the accrual accounting method, but you must file a form with the IRS called the Change in Accounting Method (Form 3115) within 180 days before the end of the tax year you want to make that change. You can find out more about the instructions for changing account method by downloading them at www.irs.gov/pub/irs-pdf/ i3115.pdf.

Q. For example, suppose you are keeping the books for a carpenter who contracted to do a job on December 15 for $15,000 and received 50 percent up front or $7,500. He spent $5,000 in cash on materials December 16 and paid his workers $5,000 in cash on December 31 when the work was completed. The contractor did not meet with the customer for final approval of the work and final payment until January 3. How would you record these transactions using the cash-basis accounting method and how would you record them using the accrual accounting method?

A. If you were keeping the books using the cash-basis accrual method, you would record the cash received on December 15 of $7,500. You would record the $5,000 cash spent on materials on December 16 and you would record the payment to workers of $5,000 cash on December 31. When you

closed your books for the year on December 31, this job would show revenues of $7,500 and expenses of $10,000 or a loss of $2,500. You would then record the $7,500 cash received on January 3 and have no corresponding expenses, so at the end of that year you would have an additional $7,500 in profits for work performed for the previous year with the expenses for the work recorded in the previous year.

If you were using the accrual method, you would record the receipt of $7,500 revenue on December 15; you would record the $5,000 cash spent on materials on December 16. You would record the payment to your workers of $5,000 in revenue on December 31. You would also record the final payment of $7,500 due in an account called Accounts Receivables, which tracks customer payments due. When you close your books at the end of the year, you would show a $5,000 profit on this job.

5. Suppose you are keeping the books for a carpenter who contracted to do a job on December 15 for $15,000 and received 50 percent up front or $7,500. He bought $5,000 of materials on store credit on December 16 and paid his workers $5,000 in cash on December 31 when the work was completed. He will not be billed for the materials until December 31 and won't pay for them with cash until January 10. While the contractor submitted a bill for the completed work on December 31, he did not meet with the customer for final approval of the work and final payment until January 3. How would you record these transactions using the cash-basis accounting method and how would you record them using the accrual accounting method? Would the job show a profit or a loss on December 31?

Solve It

6. Suppose you purchased $1,500 in products using cash on December 15 that you intend to sell to your customers. These products were completely sold out by December 25 and your total revenue for these products was $2,500, but not all of that revenue was in cash. You sold $1,500 of products and were paid with cash and $1,000 of products were sold using store credit. The customers would not be billed for that credit until January 2 and you won't receive payment until mid-January. How would you record these transactions using the cash-basis accounting method and how would you record them using the accrual accounting method? How would your revenues and expenses differ between these methods when you close the books on December 31?

Solve It

7. Suppose you purchased $1,500 in products on credit with the vendor on December 15 that you intend to sell to your customers. You won't be billed for those products until December 31 and won't have to pay for them with cash until January 10. These products were completely sold out by December 25 and your total revenue for these products was $2,500 in cash. How would you record these transactions using the cash-basis accounting method and how would you record them using the accrual accounting method? How would your revenues and expenses differ between these methods when you close the books on December 31?

Solve It

Sorting Out Assets, Liabilities, and Equity

Once you choose your accounting method, you'll next need to sort out whether items in your books are assets, liabilities, or equity. Assets include anything the company owns. Liabilities include anything the company owes. Equity reflects the money the owners have put in or taken out of the company.

In order to keep your books in balance, you need to carefully track all these different items in the right place. The key formula used in accounting for balancing the books is

Assets = Liabilities + Equity

In other words everything your business owns is balanced against claims against those items owned. Vendors and lenders, who account for most of your liabilities, have claims against the assets for the money you owe them. Owners of the business have claims against the remaining assets.

So which items fall into each of these categories? In the assets category you would find cash, marketable securities (including stocks, bonds, and money market accounts), inventory, buildings, land, equipment, and vehicles. These are all tangible assets (assets you can touch and feel). In addition to tangible assets there are intangible assets — assets that you can't touch and feel. Patents and copyrights are good examples of intangible assets. In both cases these are items a company owns based on governmental guarantees that the business has the exclusive rights to produce products based on these copyrights or patents. Another common intangible asset is organization costs, which include the initial start-up expenses of a business.

In the liabilities category you'll find bills due to vendors or suppliers, payments due to consultants, credit card bills, and bank loans. You would also find any accruals of taxes owed. There are two types of tax payments that you may accrue in a business. When you sell products to customers you collect sales taxes. When you pay your employees you collect taxes the employee owes the government including federal and state taxes, Social Security taxes, and Medicare taxes. Most small companies pay these taxes on a quarterly basis, but accrue them in a liability account until the tax is due to track future payment obligations.

In the equity category, you would find all claims that owners have against the company. If the company is incorporated, owner's claims would be reflected in a Stock account. Money paid out to stockholders would be found in a dividend expense account. If the company is privately owned, the owners claims would be reflected in a Capital account, which tracks money put into the business, and a Drawing account would track money taken out of the business by the owners. Any profits kept in the business and not paid out to owners, would be shown in a Retained Earnings account.

Q. Where in the books would you find cars owned by the company?

A. In an asset account that tracks vehicles owned by the company.

8. Where in the books would you find bills due to vendors?

Solve It

9. Where in the books would you find inventory you have on hand to sell to customers?

Solve It

10. Where in the books would you find money put into the company when the owners first started the business?

Solve It

11. Where in the books would you find the mortgage for the store that your company owns that you must pay off?

Solve It

Tracking the Daily Finances

A bookkeeper also needs to keep accurate day-to day records of business activities. These activities include maintaining inventory, tracking sales, and handling payroll.

It's critically important for any business to know what inventory it has on hand and how much that Inventory costs. The tracking of those details falls to the bookkeeper. I talk more about the bookkeeper's responsibilities in this area in Chapter 7.

Every business owner enjoys finding out how much he took in from sales of his products or services. You need to keep that data up-to-date, so the owner of the business can quickly see how well the business is doing and find trends that may indicate either an upswing or downswing in sales. If there is an upswing, the owner may need to bring in more products to sell. If there is a downswing, the owner may need to slow down his ordering to avoid having too much inventory on hand. I talk more about the bookkeeper's responsibility for tracking sales in Chapter 8.

The third critical responsibility is making sure the employees are paid accurately. You also have to be sure the government gets any taxes due related to the payroll. I talk more about managing payroll in Chapter 9.

Testing Your Work

At the end of an accounting period, you need to test to find out if you entered all the transactions in the books accurately and if your books are in balance. You start the process of testing for accuracy by proving out your cash to be sure your cash balance is accurate.

Once you know your cash is right, then you test whether your books are in balance using a trial balance. If they're not in balance you'll need to do a worksheet to find the errors and prepare journal entries to correct them. I talk more about how to test your work and make any necessary corrections at the end of an accounting period in Chapters 13 and 14.

Naming the Financial Statements

After you take the time to put all your transactions into the books, you need to have a way to summarize the financial results of all these transactions. You do that by preparing financial reports about the business's activity. Two key reports that are prepared include the Balance Sheet and Income Statement.

The Balance Sheet, which is based on the formula Assets equals Liabilities and Equity, shows a business's overall financial health at a particular date in time. The financial statement includes two columns. One lists all the assets and the second, which must be equal to the first, lists all the liabilities and equity. I show you how to prepare this statement in Chapter 15.

The Income Statement, which summarizes the activity of a business during an accounting period, shows whether the business made a profit or took a loss. The accounting period can be a month, a quarter or a year. This statement starts with the Revenues, subtracts the costs of purchasing the goods or services you sell, then subtracts the expenses incurred operating the business. The bottom line of an income statement is whether or not the company made a profit. I show you how to prepare this statement in Chapter 16.

0. On which statement and where in that statement would you find the value of the buildings owned by the company?

A. The Asset section of the Balance Sheet in an account called Buildings.

12. On which statement and where in that statement would you find the value of the mortgages due to be paid to lenders?

Solve It

13. On which statement and where in that statement would you find a business's total sales for the year?

Solve It

14. On which statement and where in that statement would you find the total amount a business spent to purchase the products it planned to sell?

Solve It

15. On which statement and where in that statement would you find the value of the inventory the company had on hand to sell to its customers?

Solve It

Keeping a Paper Trail

In addition to recording all your company's transactions in the books, you also need to keep an accurate paper trail about those transactions so if a question comes up later you have all the detail you need to provide an answer about a particular expense or revenue. It's the only way that you can track both the company's financial successes and its failures.

A company owner needs to know what succeeded, so he can repeat that success in the future and also needs to know what failed, so you can avoid repeating those errors in the future. Your books and the supporting paper trail help the business owner to do that.

There are several types of books that you keep. The granddaddy of them all is the General Ledger. This summarizes all your accounts during the year. You can imagine that there would be thousands of transactions for most businesses (large corporations have millions), so it would be unwieldy to have the details of all transactions in just one book. Instead the most active accounts are detailed in a series of journals. The monthly summary totals from the journals are then posted to the General Ledger. I talk about how General Ledgers are used in Chapter 4 and how journals are used in Chapter 5.

Many companies use computerized accounting today. In these cases the journals are kept electronically rather than on paper.

In addition to keeping the books, you also need to keep copies of the paper that was used to back up the transaction. For example, when you purchase products you intend to sell, you would get an invoice that shows how much you paid for those products. You should keep copies of all those invoices in case a question arises later. I talk more about what paperwork you need to keep and for how long you need to keep it in Chapter 6. I also talk about how to set up a filing system in that chapter, so you will be able to find everything when you need to do so.

Answers to Problems on Deciphering the Basics

1 You would record the transaction the same way using cash-basis or accrual accounting. Cash was paid on June 15, so the transaction would be recorded as a cash transaction in cash-basis accounting. The transaction was completed on June 15, so the transaction would be recorded in accrual accounting as well.

2 You would record the money due the painter on July 1 when the work is completed in the Accounts Payable account to reflect the money that is due if you are using accrual accounting. You would not record the transaction until July 5 when you pay the painter in cash using cash-basis accounting.

3 You would record the payment on July 15 when you pay with cash if you are using cash-basis accounting. If you are using accrual accounting, you would record the bill on July 1 in the Accounts Payable account if you are using accrual accounting.

4 You would record the transaction on July 15 if you are using cash-basis accounting. You would record the transaction on June 15 when you first make the sale in the Accounts Receivables account, where you track sales to customers who buy on store credit if you are using accrual accounting.

5 If you were keeping the books using cash-basis accounting, you would record the cash revenue of $7,500 on December 15. You would record the cash payment to the workers on December 31. You would record the cash revenue on January 3 and you would record the payment for materials on January 10. At the end of the year the job would show a profit of $2,500 because only $5,000 had been paid to workers and the materials were not yet paid. If you were keeping the books using accrual accounting, you would record the cash revenue of $7,500 on December 15. You would record the cash payments to workers of $5,000 on December 31. You would record the bill for materials of $5,000 on December 31, and you would also record the revenue for the completed job now due from the customer of $7,500 on December 31 in the Accounts Receivable account on December 31. At the end of the year the job would show a profit of $5,000.

6 If you were keeping the books using cash-basis accounting, you would record the $1,500 purchase of the products on December 15. You would record the cash sales of $1,500 as they were received. You would not record the sales to customers who you sold to on store credit until the money was received in mid-January. You would show $0 profit on these product sales on December 31. If you were keeping the books using an accrual accounting method, you would record the $1,500 purchase of the products on December 15. You would record the sales on the days they were made, but you would have recorded the total revenue of $2,500 by December 25. Cash sales would be recorded in the Cash account and store credit sales would be recorded in the Accounts Receivable account. You would show a profit on these product sales of $1,000 on December 31. The accrual method of accounting would show a $1,000 profit, while the cash-method would show a $0 profit.

7 If you were keeping the books using cash-basis accounting, you would record the cash sales as they were made but would total $2,500 by December 25. You would not record the cash payment of $1,500 for the products bought until you pay that bill with cash on January 10. Your revenues for these sales would total $2,500 and you wouldn't show any costs on December 31. If you were keeping the books using the accrual accounting method, you would record the sales as they were made, but would total $2,500 by December 25. You would record the bill to cover the costs of the goods on December 31 in Accounts Payable. Your revenues for these sales would total $2,500 and the costs of goods sold would total $1,500 on December 31.

8 In a liability account where you track bills called Accounts Payable.

9 In an asset account called Inventory.

10 In an equity account called Capital.

11 In a liability account called Mortgages Payable.

12 In the liability section of the Balance Sheet in a line item called Mortgages Payable.

13 In the revenues section of the Income Statement in a line item called Sales.

14 In the cost of goods sold section of the Income Statement in a line item called Purchases.

15 In the assets section of the Balance Sheet in a line item called Inventory.

Chapter 2

Designing Your Bookkeeping System

As a bookkeeper you serve as the eyes and ears of the accountant, so you have to understand the basics of accounting. In this chapter, I give you a brief overview of accounting basics and show you how to use that information to design a bookkeeping system. You also get a chance to practice the key concepts of bookkeeping design, as well as the key functions of a bookkeeping system.

Introducing the Accounts

Your role as the bookkeeper requires you to track all the financial transactions of a business. Accounting provides the structure you must use to organize these transactions, as well as the procedures you must use to record, classify, and report information about your business.

On a day-to-day basis, you make sure that all transactions are entered accurately in the books. To be a bookkeeper you must be very detail oriented and love to work with numbers. Since you spend most of your day hunched over a computer massaging the numbers, if you don't like working with numbers, forget about it — bookkeeping is not for you.

You don't have to be certified public accountant (CPA) to do the books, but for many small businesses that don't have the money to hire a full-time CPA, you will be the person who works with the accountant hired to review the books. He prepares the financial statements using the data you collected when you entered all the financial transactions.

In most cases the accounting system will be set up with the help of an accountant to be sure the information generated by that system will be useable and meets the requirements of solid accounting principals. You'll probably get periodic visits from the accountant to review your system and be sure you're entering information correctly.

A business owner is dependent upon your work to know how well his company is doing. If you put garbage into the system (inaccurate data or data entered into the wrong accounts), he will get garbage out of the system. The financial reports generated by a system with a lot of errors will be useless.

A bookkeeping system is designed based on the data needed for the two key financial reports — the balance sheet and the income statement. The balance sheet gives you a snapshot of a business as of a particular date. The income statement gives you a summary of all transactions during a particular period of time, usually a month, a quarter, or a year.

The key balance sheet accounts include

- ✔ **Assets:** Everything the business owns in order to operate successfully is considered an asset. This includes cash, buildings, land, tools, equipment, vehicles, and furniture. Each type of asset has a separate account. Another asset is the Accounts Receivable account (money due from customers who bought on credit).

- ✔ **Inventory:** Products on hand that the business plans to sell.

- ✔ **Liabilities:** All the money the company owes to others are considered liabilities. This includes unpaid bills (called Accounts Payable account), loans, and bonds. Each type of liability will have a separate account.

- ✔ **Equity:** All the money invested in the company by the owners or stock holders is considered equity. Each type of equity, and possibly each owner in a small business, will have a separate account.

The key income statement accounts include

- ✔ **Revenue:** All the money a business receives in selling its products or services is called revenue or sales and tracked in these accounts.

- ✔ **Cost of goods sold:** All money the company must spend to buy or manufacture the goods or services it sells to customers is tracked in these accounts. An account called Purchases is used to track goods purchased.

- ✔ **Expenses:** All money that is spent to run the company that is not related specifically to a product or service being sold is tracked in expenses accounts. For example, Office Supplies, Advertising, Salaries, and Wages are all types of expense accounts.

As the bookkeeper you will be responsible for identifying the account in which each transaction should be recorded. In Chapter 3, I give you a closer look at the types of accounts that fall under each of these categories.

Q. In what type of accounts would you record the sale to a customer?

a. Record both the cash and the sale in a revenue account called Sales.

b. Record the inventory sold in a liability account called Inventory; record the cash in a revenue account called Sales.

c. Record the cash in a revenue account called Sales and record the inventory sold in an asset account called Inventory.

A. The answer would be **a.** You would record the cash received in an asset account called Cash and the sale would be recorded in a revenue account called Sales.

1. In what type of accounts would you record the cash purchase of goods to be sold?

    a. Record the goods purchased in an asset account called Inventory; record the cash in an asset account called Cash.

    b. Record the goods purchased in a cost of goods sold account called Purchases; record the cash spent in an asset account called Cash.

    c. Record the goods purchased in a cost of goods sold account called Purchases; record the cash spent in a liabilities account called Cash.

    d. Record the goods purchased in an asset account called Inventory; record the cash in a liability account called Cash.

Solve It

2. In what type of accounts would you record the purchase of furniture for your office using a credit card?

    a. Record the furniture in an asset account called Furniture; record the credit card transaction in an asset account called Cash.

    b. Record the furniture in an Office Supplies expense account; record the credit card transaction in a liability account called Credit Card.

    c. Record the furniture in an asset account called Furniture; record the credit card transaction in a liability account called Credit Card.

    d. Record the furniture in an Office Supplies expense account; record the credit card transaction in an asset account called Cash.

Solve It

3. In what type of accounts would you record the payment of rent to your landlord in cash?

    a. Record the rent payment in an expense account called Rent; record the cash used in a liability account called Cash.

    b. Record the rent payment in an expense account called Rent; record the cash used in an asset account called Cash.

    c. Record the rent payment in a liability account called Rent; record the cash used in an asset account called Cash.

    d. Record the rent payment in a liability account; record the cash used in an expense account called Cash.

Solve It

In addition to learning the types of accounts and where the transactions should be recorded, you'll also need to learn an entirely new vocabulary. Some key terms you'll need to know include:

- **Accounting period:** This is the time period for which the transactions are being tracked. It can be a month, a quarter, a year or another period of time that is reasonable for the type of business. Most companies will prepare financial reports at least monthly and then prepare an annual report at the end of a 12-month accounting period.

- **Accounts Receivable:** This is where you track customer sales for customers who buy on store credit rather than pay by cash. (Read Chapter 8 for more detail about these types of transactions.)

- **Accounts Payable:** This is the account you use to track bills the company owes and has not yet paid. (Read Chapter 7 for more detail about these types of transactions.)

- **Depreciation:** This is how you track the use and aging of the equipment, furniture, buildings and other major assets the company owns. (Read Chapter 11 for more information about depreciation.)

- **General Ledger:** This summarizes all the financial transactions of a business. (Read Chapter 4 for more information about the General Ledger and how it is used.)

- **Interest:** Whenever the company borrows money, it will likely have to pay interest on the amount borrowed, just like you must do when you borrow money from the bank to buy a car or a house.

- **Inventory:** Products that the company has available for sale to its customers. (Read Chapter 7 for more information about inventory.)

- **Payroll:** All the money that is paid to the company's employees is tracked in a payroll account. (Read Chapter 9 for more detail about payroll management.)

Q. If the accountant tells you he wants to run a report that shows all the financial transactions in the last 12 months, he's asking for a report based on the:

a. Accounting period

b. Sales

c. Income

d. Profit

A. The answer would be **a,** accounting period. The account will commonly ask for a list of all transactions over a particular accounting period so he can prepare the financial statements for that period.

4. If the accountant wants to know how many products are still on the shelves after you closed the books for an accounting period, which account would you show him?

a. Cost of Goods Sold account

b. Purchases account

c. Inventory account

d. Tell him you have to count what's left in the store.

Solve It

5. If a customer buys your product on store credit, in which account would you record the transaction:

a. Accounts Payable

b. Accounts Receivable

c. Credit account

d. Would not record until the customer pays the bill

Solve It

6. You receive a bill for a new shipment of products. Where would you record that bill in the accounting system so you can pay it in the future?

a. Cost of Goods Sold account

b. Credit account

c. Accounts Payable

d. Expense account

Solve It

Cycling Through the Bookkeeping Process

In addition to understanding all the new terminology and types of accounts, as a bookkeeper you'll also need to understand how the accounting cycle works. There are eight steps in the accounting cycle:

1. **Transactions:** The process starts with financial transactions. These can include the sale or return of goods, the purchase of goods or supplies, the payment of salaries — essentially any time cash changes hands or the promise of payment is made a transaction has occurred.

2. **Journal entries:** The first thing you do after a transaction has occurred is prepare a journal entry so you can record it in the books. (Read Chapter 5 for more on journal entries.)

3. **Posting:** After preparing the journal entry you post it to the books. I discuss posting financial transactions in Chapters 4 and 5.

4. **Trial balance:** At the end of an accounting period you'll test the books to see if they are in balance. I show you how to do a trial balance in Chapter 14.

5. **Worksheet:** Often on the first try you'll find the books are not in balance. A worksheet is used to figure out the problem. I show you how to do a worksheet in Chapter 14.

6. **Adjusting journal entries:** After you figure out what is wrong, you make adjustments to the books using Adjusting Journal Entries. I show you how to prepare these entries in Chapter 14.

7. **Financial statements:** Financial statements are prepared using the corrected trial balance.

8. **Closing:** At the end of an accounting period you close the books and get ready for the next accounting period. I talk about closing the books in Chapter 18.

When you close the books, everything starts again. The accounting cycle is more like a circle than a straight line — cycling from accounting period to the next accounting period.

Q. What starts the bookkeeping cycle?

   a. Sales in the store

   b. Rental of store space

   c. Any financial transaction

   d. Paying for your business license

A. The answer would be **c.** Any financial transaction can start the bookkeeping cycle. The key is when that transaction happens. The first transaction of a new accounting period starts the bookkeeping cycle for that period, but remember once you start keeping the books the cycle is more like a continuous circle.

7. What must you prepare to enter the transaction in your books?

    a. Calculation of entry

    b. Journal entry

    c. Transaction entry

    d. Business entry

Solve It

8. How do you figure out if your books are in balance?

    a. Add up the accounts

    b. Match the balance to your checkbook

    c. Prepare a balance sheet

    d. Prepare a trial balance

Solve It

9. What type of entries do you use to correct any mistakes to get your books back in balance?

    a. Adjusting journal entries

    b. Closing entries

    c. Posting entries

    d. Correcting entries

Solve It

Seeing Double with Double-Entry Bookkeeping

Every time you enter a transaction in your books you'll be entering it twice. This is called double-entry bookkeeping and, if you do it right, your books should be in balance on the first try. Even if you do make mistakes, double-entry bookkeeping helps to minimize those mistakes and increases your chance of your books being in balance without having to make corrections.

The key to double-entry accounting and the balance of the books is this formula:

Assets = Liabilities + Equity

That's the formula for the balance sheet, which I'll talk about in greater detail in Chapter 15 after you learn all the items that are used to make up the balance sheet.

 Basically what you need to remember is that any time you enter a financial transaction, as least two accounts will be impacted by the transaction. In each entry you must have one debit and one credit. Now, you need to forget everything you ever learned about the meaning of debits and credits. From past experience you probably think of a debit as something that is subtracted from your bank account and a credit as something that is added to your bank account. You'll find debits and credits don't always work that way in accounting. For some accounts the debit will add to the account; for others it will subtract from the account. That's because it depends upon which side of the accounting formula the account is on. I talk more about how to figure this out in the section, "Differentiating Between Debits and Credits" later in this chapter.

First, I want you to practice the basics of developing a double entry. For example, suppose you bought furniture using cash totaling $1,000. You spent cash to buy the furniture, but you also added a new asset.

 Q. How would you develop a journal entry to enter this financial transaction in your books?

A. Here is what the transaction would look like:

Account	Debit	Credit
Furniture	$1,000	
Cash		$1,000

So how does this impact the accounting equation? Both accounts are asset accounts, so a debit to the Furniture account will increase the ending balance of that account. The credit to the Cash account will decrease the total balance of the Cash account. So the total value of the assets would not change and would keep the asset side of the equation equal to the liabilities and equity side.

Before getting into the impact of each of these transactions on the account, first try developing these journal entries:

10. You buy new products to be sold in your store on credit for $3,000. How would you enter this transaction in your books?

Solve It

Account	Debit	Credit

11. You sold $5,000 worth of goods and received $5,000 in cash. How would you enter it in your books?

Solve It

Account	Debit	Credit

12. You sold $3,000 worth of goods on store credit. You didn't get cash. Customers will pay you after you bill them. How will your record the sales transaction?

Solve It

Account	Debit	Credit

13. You buy office supplies for $500 using a check. How would you record the transaction?

Solve It

Account	Debit	Credit

Differentiating Between Debits and Credits

When first starting to use debits and credits, the hardest thing for most people to learn is whether a debit increases or decreases an account and whether a credit increases or decreases an account. It all depends on the type of account. As you learn how all this works, copy and tape Table 2-1 somewhere handy — you should keep a copy at your desk.

Table 2-1	How Credits and Debits Impact Your Accounts	
Account Type	*Debits*	*Credits*
Assets	Increase	Decrease
Liabilities	Decrease	Increase
Income	Decrease	Increase
Expenses	Increase	Decrease

Q. How would you develop a journal entry to enter the financial transaction from the previous example in your books?

A. Here is what the transaction would look like:

Account	*Debit*	*Credit*
Furniture	$1,000	
Cash		$1,000

As mentioned above, the Furniture account will increase the ending balance of that account. The credit to the Cash account will decrease the total balance of the Cash account. So the total value of the assets would not change and would keep the assets equal to the liabilities and equity.

I want you to revisit the four transactions you completed above and indicate what will happen to the balance of the accounts in each of these transactions.

14. You buy new products to be sold in your store on credit for $3,000. Copy the journal entry you developed above and then indicate whether the transaction action would increase or decrease the accounts involved.

Solve It

Account   *Debit*   *Credit*

15. You sold $5,000 worth of goods and received $5,000 in cash. Copy the journal entry you developed above and then indicate whether the transaction action would increase or decrease the accounts involved.

Solve It

Account   *Debit*   *Credit*

16. You sold $3,000 worth of goods on store credit. You didn't get cash. Customers will pay you after you bill them. Copy the journal entry you developed above and then indicate whether the transaction action would increase or decrease the accounts involved.

Solve It

Account   *Debit*   *Credit*

17. You buy office supplies using a check. Copy the journal entry you developed above and then indicate whether the transaction action would increase or decrease the accounts involved.

Solve It

Account   *Debit*   *Credit*

Answers to Problems on Designing Your Bookkeeping System

1 **B:** Record the goods purchased in a cost of goods sold account called Purchases; record the cash spent in an asset account. You would not record the goods purchased in the Inventory account. Inventory is adjusted at the end of an accounting period after a physical count of the inventory has been done. The one exception to this is a business that does computerized management of its inventory system. In most cases when inventory is computerized, the system automatically adjusts inventory with each purchase of goods. But even with this type of system the initial entry would be to the Purchases account and the computer would then automatically update the Inventory account.

2 **C:** Record the furniture in an asset account called Furniture, record the credit card transaction in a liability account called Credit Card. You would record the charge on the credit card in a liability account called Credit Card. Cash would not be paid until the credit card bill is due to be paid. Furniture is always listed as an asset on your balance sheet. Anything you buy that you expect to use for more than one year will be an asset rather then an expense.

3 **B:** Record the rent payment in an expense account called Rent; record the cash used in an asset account called Cash. Cash is always an asset account. It does not matter whether or not you are taking cash out to buy something or depositing cash you received after making a sale. Rent is always an expense.

4 **C:** Inventory Account. The Inventory account is adjusted at the end of each accounting period to show the total number of products remaining to be sold at the end of the accounting period.

5 **B:** Accounts Receivable. The Accounts Receivable is the account that is used to track all customer purchases made by store credit. In addition to this account that summarizes all products bought on credit, you would also need to enter the purchases into the individual accounts of each of your customers so you can bill them and track their payments.

6 **C:** Accounts Payable. All bills that will be due at some time in the future are tracked in the Accounts Payable account.

7 **C:** Journal entry. When you prepare the journal entry, you take the time to think about the accounts impacted by the transaction. There will always be at least two accounts in the entry — one a debit and one a credit.

8 **D:** Prepare a trial balance. The trial balance is a working tool that helps you test whether your books are in balance before you prepare your financial statements.

9 **A:** Adjusting Journal Entries. At the end of an accounting period you correct any mistakes using Adjusting Journal Entries. These entries will also need to be in balance. You will always have at least one account that is a debit and one that is a credit.

10 In this transaction you would debit the Purchases account to show the additional purchases made during that period and credit the Accounts Payable account. Since you are buying the goods on credit that means you will have to pay the bill at some point in the future.

Account	Debit	Credit
Purchases	$3,000	
Accounts Payable		$3,000

11 As you think about the journal entry you may not know whether something is a credit or a debit. As you know from our discussions earlier in the chapter, a debit to the Cash account increases the balance in that account. In this question since you did receive cash, you know that the Cash account needs to be a debit. So your only choice is to make the Sales account the account to be credited. All income accounts are increased by a credit. If you are having trouble figuring this out, use the chart at the end of the chapter to become familiar with which accounts are increased by a credit or a debit and which accounts are decreased by a debit or a credit.

Account	Debit	Credit
Cash	$5,000	
Sales		$5,000

12 In this question, rather than taking in cash, the customers were allowed to pay on credit, so you need to debit the asset account Accounts Receivable. You will credit the Sales account to track the additional revenue.

Account	Debit	Credit
Accounts Receivable	$3,000	
Sales		$3,000

13 In this question since you are paying with a check, it will be recorded in your Cash account. The Cash account tracks the amount in your bank account. Any cash, checks, debit cards or other types of transactions that will be taken directly from you bank account will always be entered as a credit. All money paid out for expenses will always be a debit.

Account	Debit	Credit
Office Supplies	$500	
Cash		$500

14 In this transaction the debit would increase the balance of the Purchases account to show the additional money spent and the credit would increase the balance of the Accounts Payable account to show the additional bill that must be paid at some point in the future.

Account	Debit	Credit
Purchases	$3,000	
Accounts Payable		$3,000

15 The Cash account balance would be increased to show the newly received cash and the Sales account would be increased to show the new sales.

Account	Debit	Credit
Cash	$5,000	
Sales		$5,000

16 The Accounts Receivable account balance would be increased to show the new customer purchases that will be paid at some point in the future. The Sales account would be increased to show the new sales.

Account	Debit	Credit
Accounts Receivable	$3,000	
Sales		$3,000

17 The Office Supplies account balance would be increased to show the additional expenses. The Cash account would be decreased to track the use of cash.

Account	Debit	Credit
Office Supplies	$500	
Cash		$500

Chapter 3

Sorting Out Your Business Road Map

In This Chapter

▶ Mapping out the accounts

▶ Allocating your assets and liabilities

▶ Itemizing your income

*B*ookkeepers need a roadmap that helps them determine where to put the numbers. By developing a Chart of Accounts with clearly defined places for all your transactions, you can produce financial statements that will accurately reflect your businesses activities for the year. This chapter will introduce you to what goes into developing a chart of accounts and how to set it up.

Charting Your Accounts

A Chart of Accounts is organized to make it easier for you to produce two key financial statements:

✔ The balance sheet, which shows what your business owns and what it owes

✔ The income statement, which shows how much money your business took in (revenue) and how much money it spent to generate those sales (expenses)

You can find out more about balance sheets in Chapter 15 and income statements in Chapter 16. The Chart of Accounts should always start with the accounts you need to produce a balance sheet and then follow with accounts you need to produce an income statement.

The basic order for your Chart of Accounts should start by listing the balance sheet accounts:

✔ **Current Assets:** Accounts for tracking everything the company owns and expects to use in the next 12 months, including cash, accounts receivable (money collected from customers), inventory, and any other current assets with a lifespan of less than a year.

✔ **Long-term Assets:** Accounts for tracking things the company owns that have a lifespan of more than 12 months, such as buildings, furniture, and equipment.

✔ **Current Liabilities:** Accounts for tracking debts the company must pay over the next 12 months, such as accounts payable (bills from vendors, contractors, and consultants), interest payable, and credit cards payable.

✔ **Long-term Liabilities:** Accounts for tracking debts the company must pay over a period of time longer than the next 12 months, such as mortgages payable and bonds payable.

✔ **Equity:** Accounts for tracking company owners and their claims against the company's assets, which includes any money invested in the company, any money taken out of the company, and any earnings that have been reinvested in the company.

The rest of the chart is filled with income statement accounts, which you list in this order:

- ✔ **Revenue:** Accounts for tracking sales of goods and services as well as revenue generated for the company by other means
- ✔ **Cost of Goods Sold:** Accounts for tracking the direct costs involved in selling the company's goods or services
- ✔ **Expenses:** Accounts for tracking expenses related to running the businesses that aren't directly tied to the sale of individual products or services

Q. In what section of the Chart of the Accounts would you list the account named Cash?

a. Current Assets

b. Long-term Assets

c. Current Liabilities

d. Equity

A. The answer would be **a,** Current Assets. Cash would always be the first account that appears in your Chart of Accounts. It is always assumed that cash will be used in the next 12 months.

---

1. In what section of the Chart of Accounts would you list the account called Inventory?

a. Current Assets

b. Long-term Assets

c. Cost of Goods Sold

d. Expenses

Solve It

2. In what section of your Chart of Accounts would you list the account called Sales?

a. Current Assets

b. Revenue

c. Equity

d. Long-term Assets

Solve It

3. In what section of the Chart of Accounts would you list the account called Advertising?

    a. Current Liabiltiies

    b. Long-term Liabiilties

    c. Cost of Goods Sold

    d. Expenses

Solve It

4. In what section of the Chart of Accounts would you list the account called Purchases?

    a. Current Liabiltiies

    b. Long-term Liabiilties

    c. Cost of Goods Sold

    d. Expenses

Solve It

Detailing Your Balance Sheet Accounts

First, I want to take a closer look at the types of Balance Sheet accounts you would have in each of the five Asset sections of the Chart of Accounts — Current Assets, Long-term Assets, Current Liabilities, Long-term Liabilities, and Equity. Then I will give you space to jot down your own list of Balance Sheet accounts for your business. Whatever you write down now is not carved in stone. You can add to and subtract from the Chart of Accounts. You can add an account at any time of the year, but you should only subtract accounts at the end of an accounting period to be sure you don't lost any transactions with the deletion.

Current Assets

When thinking about the types of accounts you want to list as current assets, think about things your business owns that you expect will be used up in the next 12 months. Here are the most common types of current asset accounts:

    ✔ **Cash in Checking:** Your company's primary account that is used to deposit revenues and pay expenses would be tracked in this account. You may have more than one cash operating account if your company has several divisions each with their own Cash in Checking account.

- ✓ **Cash in Savings:** Your company would use this account for surplus cash. Cash for which you have no immediate plans at the very least should be deposited in an interest-earning savings account until the company decides what to do with it.

- ✓ **Cash on Hand:** Your company would use this account to track any petty cash or cash kept in store cash registers.

- ✓ **Accounts Receivable:** If you offer your products or services to customers on store credit given by your company, then you need this account to track the customers who buy on credit, so you can collect from them at a later date.

- ✓ **Inventory:** You track all products you have on hand to sell to your customers.

You may also want to set up asset accounts for items that you prepay, such as insurance, which is usually paid for an entire year. You would track it as a current asset and gradually reduce its value as you allocate it as an expense month to month. This would be called Prepaid Insurance. I talk more about how to handle prepaid items in Chapter 14.

Try It

Exercise 3-1: Think about the current assets you will need to track for your business, and write down the accounts in this section.

Long-Term Assets

When thinking about the types of accounts you want to list as long-term assets, think about the things your company owns that you will use for more than 12 months. Here are some common Long-term Asset accounts:

- ✓ **Land:** You can track any land owned by the company in this account.

- ✓ **Buildings:** You can track the value of any buildings owned by the company in this account.

✔ **Leasehold Improvements:** If your company leases any facilities, you track the value of any improvements that you did to this leased space in this account. For example, if you lease a retail store, any improvements that you make to customize this space for your business would be traced in this account.

✔ **Vehicles:** Any vehichles your company owns would be tracked in this account.

✔ **Furniture and Fixtures:** You track any furniture or fixtures purchased for use in the business in this account.

✔ **Equipment:** You track any equipment that was purchased for use for more than one year, such as computers, copiers, tools, and cash registers in this account.

In addition to these accounts, each long-term asset account will have an accumulated depreciation account to reflect the portion of the asset that already has been used up. I talk more about depreciation in Chapter 11.

Try It

Exercise 3-2: Think about the long-term asset accounts you will need to track for your business, and write down the accounts for those assets in this section.

Current Liabilities

Current liabilities are debts due in the next 12 months. Some of the most common types of Current Liabilities accounts that appear on the Chart of Accounts include:

✔ **Accounts Payable:** You should track any money the company owes to vendors, contractors, suppliers, and consultants that must be paid in the next 12 months in this account.

✔ **Sales Tax Collected:** You may not think of sales tax as a liability, but because the business collects taxes from customers and doesn't pay them immediately to the government, the taxes collected become a liability tracked in this account.

✔ **Accrued Payroll Taxes:** You should use this account to track payroll taxes collected from employees to pay state, local, or federal income taxes as well as Social Security and Medicare taxes.

✔ **Credit Cards Payable:** You should track all your company's credit card accounts to which the business is liable.

How you set up your current liabilities and how many individual accounts you establish depends upon how detailed you want to track each type of liability. For example, you can set up a separate Current Liability account for each of your major vendors if you find that approach provides you with a better money management tool.

Try It

_____

Exercise 3-3: Think about the Current Liabilites accounts you will need to track for your business, and write down the accounts for those liabiliites in this section.

Long-Term Liabilities

Long-term liabilities include any debts that are due in more than 12 months. The number of Long-term Liabilities accounts you maintain on your Chart of Accounts depends on your debt structure. The two most common types of long-term liability accounts are

✔ **Loans Payable:** You use this account to track any long-term loans, such as a mortgage on your business building. Most businesses have separate loans payable accounts for each of their long-term loans. For example, you could have Loans Payable – Mortgage Bank for your building and Loans Payable – Car Bank for your vehicle loan.

✔ **Notes Payable:** Some businesses borrow money from other businesses using notes, a method of borrowing that doesn't require the company to put up an asset, such as a mortgage on a building or a car loan, as collateral. This account tracks any notes due.

In addition to any separate Long-term Debt accounts you may want to track in their own account, you may also want to set up an account called "Other Liabilities." You would use this account to track debt that you don't think needs its own individual account.

Try It

Exercise 3-4: Think about the Long-term Liabilities accounts you will need to track for your business, and write down the accounts for those liabilities in this section.

Equity

Every business is owned by somebody. Equity accounts track owners' contributions to the business as well as their share of ownership. For a corporation, ownership is tracked by the sale of individual shares of stock because each stockholder owns a portion of the business. In smaller companies that are owned by one person or a group of people, equity is tracked using Capital and Drawing accounts. Here are the basic Equity accounts that appear in the Chart of Accounts:

✔ **Common Stock:** If your company is structured as a corporation, then the value of outstanding shares of stock that were sold to investors would be tracked in this account.

✔ **Retained Earnings:** Whether or not your company is incorporated, use this account to track any earnings that were kept in the business.

✔ **Capital:** You use this account if you are keeping the books for a small, unincorporated business. The Capital account reflects the amount of initial money the business owner contributed to the company as well as other owner contributions made after initial start-up.

✔ **Drawing:** This account is another that will be necessary if you are keeping the books for a small, unincorporated business. The Drawing account tracks any money that a business owner takes out of the business. If the business has several partners, each partner gets his or her own Drawing account to track what he or she takes out of the business.

Try It

_____

Exercise 3-5: Think about the Equity accounts you will need to track for your business, and write down the accounts you will need in this section.

Tracking Your Income Accounts

The Income Statement shows whether or not your business made a profit. Accounts that you set up to produce this statement can be grouped into three types of accounts:

✔ **Revenue:** These accounts track all money coming into the business, including sales, interest earned on savings, and any other methods used to generate income.

✔ **Cost of Goods Sold**: These accounts track the money spent to manufacture or buy the products you sell.

✔ **Expenses:** These accounts track all money that a business spends in order to keep itself afloat.

This section examines the various accounts that make up the Income Statement portion of the Chart of Accounts. You always start by listing the Revenue accounts, followed by the Cost of Goods Sold accounts and then the Expenses accounts.

Revenue

In the revenue section, the accounts you set up will track all money taken into the business from sales. If you choose to offer discounts or accept returns, that activity also falls in this section. The most common income accounts are

- **Sales of Goods or Services:** You track all the money that the company earns selling its products, services, or both in this account.

- **Sales Discounts:** If you offer sales discounts, you track any reductions to the full price of merchandise in this account.

- **Sales Returns:** Every business ends up needing to accept returns from customers. You track any returns from customers in this account.

- **Other Income:** If your company takes in income from a source other then its primary business activity, you should record that income in this account. For example, suppose you decide to encourage recycling and earn income from the items recycled, record that income in this account.

Try It

Exercise 3-6: Think about the Revenue accounts you will need to track for your business, and write down those accounts in this section.

Cost of Goods Sold

Before you can sell a product, you must spend some money to either buy or make that product. You track these costs in accounts in the Cost of Goods Sold category. The most common Cost of Goods Sold accounts include

- **Purchases:** Track all purchases of products in this account.

- **Purchase Discount:** If you get discounts on what you purchase, track them in this account. For example, a company may give you a 2 percent discount on your purchase if you pay the bill in 10 days rather than wait until the end of the 30-day payment allotment.

- **Purchase Returns:** If you're unhappy with a product you've bought, record the value of any returns in this account.

- **Freight Charges:** Any charges related to shipping items you purchase for later sale are tracked in this account.

- **Other Sales Costs:** Use this account for any costs that don't fit into one of the other Cost of Goods Sold accounts.

Try It

Exercise 3-7: Think about the Cost of Goods Sold accounts you will need to track for your business, and write down those accounts in this section.

Expenses

Your longest list of individual accounts will be the Expense accounts. Any money you spend on the business that can't be tied directly to the sale of an individual product falls under the Expense account category. For example, advertising a storewide sale isn't directly tied to the sale of any one product, so the costs associated with advertising fall under the Expense account category. The most common Expense accounts include

- ✔ **Advertising:** Tracks all expenses involved in promoting a business or its products. In this account money spent on newspaper, television, magazine, and radio advertising is recorded as well as any money spent to print flyers and mailings to customers. Also, when a company participates in community events such as cancer walks or craft fairs, associated costs are tracked in this account as well.

- ✔ **Bank Service Charges:** Use this account to track any charges made by a bank to service a company's bank accounts.

- ✔ **Dues and Subscriptions:** Use this account to track expenses related to business club membership or subscriptions to magazines for the business.

- ✔ **Equipment Rental:** Use this account to track expenses related to renting equipment for a short-term project. For example, if you need to rent a truck to pick up some new fixtures for the store, record that truck rental in this account.

- ✔ **Insurance:** Use this account to track expenses for buying insurance.

- ✔ **Legal and Accounting:** Use this account to track money paid for legal or accounting advice.

- ✔ **Miscellaneous Expenses:** Use this account for expenses that don't fit in other accounts. If you start recording expenses in this account and later decide you want to track them individually in their own account, you can choose to add an account to the Chart of Accounts and move related expenses into that new account by subtracting all related transactions from the Miscellaneous Expenses account and adding them to the new account. With this movment of transactions, it's important to carefully balance out the adjusting transaction to avoid any errors or double counting.

- ✔ **Office Expense:** Use this account to track any items purchased in order to run an office. For example, office supplies such as paper and pens or business cards fit in this account.

- ✔ **Payroll Taxes:** Use this account to track any taxes paid related to employee payroll, such as the employer's share of Social Security and Medicare, unemployment compensation, and workman's compensation.

- ✔ **Postage:** Use this account to track any money spent on stamps, express package shipping, and other shipping.

- ✔ **Rent Expense:** Use this account to track rental costs for a business's office or retail space.

- ✔ **Salaries and Wages:** Use this account to track any money paid to employees as salary or wages.

- ✔ **Supplies:** Use this account to track any business supplies that don't fit into the category of office supplies. For example, supplies needed for the operation of retail stores are tracked using this account.

- ✔ **Travel and Entertainment:** Use this account to track money spent for business purposes for travel or entertainment. Some businesses separate these expenses into several accounts, such as Travel and Entertainment; Meals, Travel and Entertainment; Travel, and Travel and Entertainment; Entertainment to keep a close watch.

✔ **Telephone:** Use this account to track all business expenses related to the telephone and telephone calls.

✔ **Utilities:** Use this account to track money paid for utilities, such as electricity, gas, and water.

✔ **Vehicles:** Use this account to track expenses related to the operation of company vehicles.

Try It

Exercise 3-8: Think about the Expense accounts you will need to track for your business, and write down those accounts in this section.

Setting Up Your Accounts Road Map

Use the lists you just developed to set up your Chart of Accounts. You can see there really isn't a secret to how these Chart of Accounts are set up. You set them up based on how you believe your business will operate.

Your Chart of Accounts is not carved in stone. This is a chart that you can regularly update as your business grows and changes. But, you should be very careful about adding and subtracting accounts in the middle of an accounting period.

If you want to add an account, you can do so at any time, but be sure you carefully transfer the funds from the old account in which you were posting the transactions to the new account you decide to set up. You do this with what is called an adjusting journal entry. I talk more about adjusting entries amd reworking your Chart of

Accounts in Chapter 14. If you want to delete an account, indicate in your books that no new transactions should be added to that account, but wait until the end of the year to delete the account.

When you set up the Chart of Accounts, plan for three columns. The column heads would be

- **Account:** List all accounts by name.
- **Type:** List the type of account, such as asset, liability, equity, income, cost of goods sold, expense.
- **Description:** Describe the types of transactions that will be posted to that account.

Here is the basic format for the Chart of Accounts:

Account	Type	Description
Cash in Checking	Asset	Tracks all use of cash through transactions in the company's checking account

You should include as much detail as you need when describing the accounts, so that all employees who are involved in entering transactions in the books or coding a transaction to be entered into the books will know which account to specify for the transaction. If transactions are not entered consistently, your financial reports won't be accurate.

Answers to Problems on Sorting Out Your Business Road Map

1 **A:** Current Assets. Inventory is considered an asset that will be used up in the next 12 months. It is not an Expense or Cost of Goods Sold account. When inventory is actually purchased it is recorded in the Purchases account, but the Inventory account tracks that inventory on hand in the warehouse or on the store shelves at the end of an accounting period. To find out more about inventory and how to track it, read Chapter 7.

2 **B:** Revenue. All money taken into the business from the sale of your products or services would be recorded in Revenue accounts.

3 **D:** Expenses. Advertising is an expense because it usually involves the promotion of more than just one individual item to be sold. Advertising draws people into the business with the hopes of selling other items as well, so advertising transactions are not recorded in Cost of Goods Sold accounts.

4 **C:** Costs of Goods Sold. As indicated in the answer to question 1, purchases of inventory are recorded in Cost of Goods Sold accounts.

The remaining exercises in the chapter did not have right or wrong answers. You should set up your Chart of Accounts with accounts that match how your business operates.

Part II
Putting it All on Paper

The 5th Wave   By Rich Tennant

"This ledger certainly paints a picture of the
company. Edvard Munch's 'The Scream'
comes to mind."

In this part . . .

You'll find the structure for entering business transactions into your books a bit weird at first, but there is a method to the madness that will help you keep your books in balance. I introduce you to the method used to correctly enter your financial transactions, how to post transactions to your General Ledger (the granddaddy of your bookkeeping system) and how to track all the transaction details in your journals.

Chapter 4

Looking at the Big Picture

. . . .

. . . .

Accountants and bookkeepers need one place they can go to review a summary of all business transactions during an accounting period and get a look at the big picture. The General Ledger is that place.

This chapter introduces you to the General Ledger and how it is used. You will practice how to create your own entries and how to post them to the General Ledger.

Preparing the Core of Your Financial Details

Think of the General Ledger as the core of a wide network of financial data. The accounts in the General Ledger are based on your Chart of Accounts. Because it does include at least a summary of all financial transactions, the General Ledger would become too massive and unwieldy if every piece of financial data was stored in that core.

Instead many of the details about your financial transactions are stored in journals, which I discuss in greater detail in Chapter 5. Most of the key entries in the General Ledger are summaries of daily or monthly activity posted from one of the key journals where daily financial transactions are recorded.

The most common journals include the Cash Disbursements Journal (tracks the daily use of cash), Cash Receipts Journal (tracks daily cash received), Sales Journal (tracks day to day sales), Purchases Journal (tracks purchases of products for sale), and the General Journal (tracks miscellaneous financial transactions that are not tracked in their own journal). Now this is by no means an exhaustive list of all the possible journals a business might have, but they are the five main ones. Each company determines the level of detail it wants to keep and how many different journals will be kept.

If your company has computerized your bookkeeping system, the journals are automatically generated by the system as you enter financial transactions into the computer. You can view the journals on the screen or print out them out.

Q. In which journal would you record a cash receipt of $500?

    a. Cash Receipts Journal

    b. General Journal

    c. Cash Disbursements Journal

    d. Purchases Journal

A. Cash Receipts Journal

1. In which journal would you record the purchase of new furniture for the store on credit?

    a. Purchases Journal

    b. General Journal

    c. Cash Disbursements Journal

    d. Cash Receipts Journal

Solve It

2. In which journal would you record the payment of bills with cash?

    a. Purchases Journal

    b. General Journal

    c. Cash Disbursements Journal

    d. Cash Receipts Journal

Solve It

3. In which journal would you record the sale of goods to a customer on credit?

a. General Journal

b. Sales Journal

c. Cash Disbursements Journal

d. Cash Receipts Journal

Solve It

Developing Entries for the Ledger

Since you enter much of your financial transaction data into journals, you're probably wondering how the information makes it into the General Ledger. At the end of each month you total the entries in each journal and develop summary entries for the General Ledger. As you develop each entry for the General Ledger, you must be sure the entry is in balance, which means the total of your debits must equal the total of your credits.

In Figure 4-1, I show you a sample page from a Purchases Journal. You can see that there is a column for the date of the transaction, the vendor, an invoice number, a Purchases debit, and an Accounts Payable credit. Each time products are purchased for sale the debit to the Purchases account will increase the amount of money spent on Purchases and the credit to the Accounts Payable account will increase the amount of money owed to vendors.

At the end of the month when it is time to develop an entry for the General Ledger, the Purchases Journal columns will be totaled. Then a summary entry will developed based on those totals.

Figure 4-1:
Sample page from a Purchases Journal showing total purchases for the month of May for a fictitious company, ABC Candy Shop.

		ABC Candy Shop				
		Purchases Journal				
		May 2007				

Date	Vendor	Invoice Number	Purchases Debit	Accounts Payable Credit	
5 1	Ruth's Sweets	1780 -	2000 -	2000 -	
5 10	Henry's Packaging Supplies	1525 -	1500 -	1500 -	
5 15	Deb's Paper Goods	360 -	575 -	575 -	
5 25	Karen's Grocery	2570 -	175 -	175 -	
			4250 -	4250 -	

Q. Using the information in Figure 4-1, how would you develop an entry for the General Ledger to record information from the Purchases Journal for the month of May?

A. Note that you only need to record the totals for the transactions that month in the General Ledger. You don't have to record all the information.

Account	Debit	Credit
Purchases	$4,250	
Accounts Payable		$4,250

Figure 4-2:
Sample page from a Sales Journal showing total sales for the month of May for a fictitious company, ABC Candy Shop.

		ABC Candy Shop				
		Sales Journal				
		May 2007				

Date	Customer	Invoice Number	Accounts Receivable Debit	Sales Credit	
5 1	S. Smith	321 -	75 -	75 -	
5 7	John's Shop	322 -	250 -	250 -	
5 15	Pam's Shop	323 -	175 -	175 -	
5 20	Harry's Hotel	324 -	1550 -	1550 -	
5 25	Len's Restraunt	325 -	1325 -	1325 -	
			3375 -	3375 -	

4. Using the information in Figure 4-2, how would you develop an entry for the General Ledger to record transactions from the Sales Journal for the month of May?

Solve It

Figure 4-3:
Sample
page for a
Cash
Disburse-
ments
Journal for
the month of
May for a
fictitious
company,
ABC Candy
Shop.

Figure 4-3:
Sample
page for a
Cash
Disburse-
ments
Journal for
the month of
May for a
fictitious
company,
ABC Candy
Shop.

ABC Candy Shop
Cash Disbursements Journal
May 2007

Date	Account	General Debit	Accounts Payable Debit	Salaries Debit	Cash Credit
5 1	Rent	1500—			1500—
5 3	Acct. Payable- Joe's Supplies		1250—		1250—
5 4	Acct. Payable- Ruth's Sweets		2000—		2000—
5 10	Salaries			800—	800—
5 20	Credit Card Payment	550—			550—
					6100—

5. Using the information from Figure 4-3, how would you develop an entry for the General Ledger to record transactions from the Cash Disbursements Journal for the month of May?

Solve It

Figure 4-4:
Sample
page for a
General
Journal for
the month of
May for a
fictitious
company,
ABC Candy
Shop.

ABC Candy Shop
General Journal
May 2007

Date	Account	General Debit	General Credit	Accounts Payable Debit	Accounts Receivable
5 6	Sales Return	25 -			
	S. Smith				25 -
	Credit Memo 134				
5 15	Henry's Packing			450 -	
	Purchase Return		450 -		
	Debit Memo 1235				
5 20	Deb's Paper Goods			100 -	
	Purchase Return		100 -		
	Debit Memo 256				
5 25	Office Furniture	700 -			
	(Inv. 1236)		700 -		
	Credit Card Payable				

6. Using the information from Figure 4-4, how would you develop an entry for the General Ledger to record transactions from the General Journal for the month of May?

Solve It

Posting Your Entries

After you develop your entries, you need to post them to the accounts in the General Ledger. When you post entries to the General Ledger, you must make sure you can track back those entries to their original location in the books. For example, if you are posting an entry that summarizes activity from the Purchases Journal, you would want to include a reference to the page in that journal from which the summary was taken. That way if there are any questions about an entry posted to the General Ledger, you have a way of tracing the source of the posted information and researching any questions that arise.

Q. The entry developed for the General Ledger from the summary on Page 2 of the Purchases Journal on May 31 was

Account	Debit	Credit
Purchases	$4,250	
Accounts Payable		$4,250

How would you record the entry into the General Ledger accounts of Purchases and Accounts Payable?

A. Review Figures 4-5 and 4-6 to see how these entries would be posted to General Ledger accounts.

Each account in the General Ledger will have a separate page or pages. Entries will be made from journals or directly to the General Ledger throughout the month. At the end of the month the account balance will be totaled. I talk more about how to close the books out at the end of the month or end of another accounting period, such as a quarter or year, in Chapter 13.

You can see that the date of the entry is placed in the first column. Next you will find a description indicating the source of the entry, followed by a reference number (which for a journal entry would be the page of the journal on which it is found); then you would post any debits to the debit column and any credits to the credit column.

Figure 4-5:
Sample of a
General
Ledger page
for the
Purchases
account.

ABC Candy Shop
Purchases
May 2007

Date	Description	Ref. No.	Debit	Credit	Balance
5 1	Opening Balance				- 0 -
5 31	From Purchases Journal	Page 2	4200 -		

Figure 4-6:
Sample of a
General
Ledger page
for the
Accounts
Payable
account.

ABC Candy Shop
Accounts Payable
May 2007

Date	Description	Ref. No.	Debit	Credit	Balance
5 1	Opening Balance				2000 -
5 31	From Purchases Journal	Page 2		4200 -	

7. How would you post this journal entry developed using the information on page 2 of the Sales Journal on May 31 to the General Ledger:

Account	Debit	Credit
Accounts Receivable	$3,375	
Sales		$3,375

Solve It

Accounts Receivable

Date	Description	Ref. No.	Debit	Credit	Balance

Sales

Date	Description	Ref. No.	Debit	Credit	Balance

8. How would you post this journal entry developed using the information on page 3 of the Cash Disbursements Journal on May 31 to the General Ledger:

Account	Debit	Credit
Rent	$1,500	
Accounts Payable	$3,250	
Credit Card Payable	$550	
Salaries	$800	
Cash		$6,100

Solve It

Rent Expenses

Date	Description	Ref. No.	Debit	Credit	Balance

Accounts Payable

Date	Description	Ref. No.	Debit	Credit	Balance

Credit Card Payable

Date	Description	Ref. No.	Debit	Credit	Balance

Salaries

Date	Description	Ref. No.	Debit	Credit	Balance

Cash

Date	Description	Ref. No.	Debit	Credit	Balance

9. How would you post this journal entry developed using the information on page 5 of the General Journal on May 31 to the General Ledger:

Account	Debit	Credit
Sales Return	$25	
Accounts Payable	$550	
Office Furniture	$700	
Purchases Return		$550
Credit Card Payable		$700
Accounts Receivable		$25

Solve It

Sales Return

Date	Description	Ref. No.	Debit	Credit	Balance

Accounts Payable

Date	Description	Ref. No.	Debit	Credit	Balance

Credit Card Payable

Date	Description	Ref. No.	Debit	Credit	Balance

Purchases Return

Date	Description	Ref. No.	Debit	Credit	Balance

Accounts Receivable

Date	Description	Ref. No.	Debit	Credit	Balance

Office Furniture

Date	Description	Ref. No.	Debit	Credit	Balance

Adjusting for Errors

Entries that you make into the General Ledger are not cast in stone. You can always adjust those entries. I talk more about how to do that in Chapter 14. Three of the most common reasons for making an adjusting entry include

- ✓ **Depreciation:** This shows how an asset is being used up and allocates the cost of using that asset over the life of the asset. I talk more about depreciation in Chapter 11. Most companies post adjusting entries for depreciation once a year, but it can be done more frequently.

- ✓ **Prepaid expenses:** Expenses that you must prepay, such as a 12-month premium on an insurance policy, are expensed on a monthly basis using an adjusting entry. I talk more about how to do that in Chapter 14.

- ✓ **Adding an account:** When an account is added, you may need to move some transactions that were posted in one account to the new account. You do this using an adjusting entry, removing the dollar amount from the account where it was first posted, and then entering the amount into the new account. I talk more about this process in Chapter 14.

Answers to Problems on Looking at the Big Picture

1 **B:** General Journal. The purchase of new furniture for the store would actually be an asset and not a cost for the purpose of purchasing or manufacturing items for sale. Therefore, you would not put it in the Purchases Journal, but instead in the journal for miscellaneous entries — the General Journal.

2 **C:** Cash Disbursements Journal. All cash payments are entered into the Cash Disbursements Journal.

3 **B:** Sales Journal. All sales are tracked in the Sales Journal.

4 See the following table for the answer:

Account	Debit	Credit
Accounts Receivable	$3,375	
Sales		$3,375

5 See the following table for the answer:

Account	Debit	Credit
Rent	$1,500	
Accounts Payable	$3,250	
Credit Card Payable	$550	
Salaries	$800	
Cash		$6,100

6 Note that in this case the accounts that were posted to a specific company are not listed. A Purchase Return is a product that you intended to sell but returned to a vendor. Therefore, you reduce the amount you owe that vendor by debiting Accounts Payable, which would reduce the amount due in Accounts Payable. When a customer returns a product to you, you must reduce the amount the customer owes. You would not only reduce the amount in that customer's account, but you would also credit Accounts Receivable where you track payments due from customers.

Account	Debit	Credit
Sales Return	$25	
Accounts Payable	$550	
Office Furniture	$700	
Purchase Return		$550
Credit Card Payable		$700
Accounts Receivable		$25

7 Here is how you would post the information to the Accounts Receivable and Sales accounts of the General Ledger:

Accounts Receivable

Date	Description	Ref. No.	Debit	Credit	Balance
5/31	From the Sales Journal	Page 2	$3,375		

Sales

Date	Description	Ref. No.	Debit	Credit	Balance
5/31	From the Sales Journal	Page 2		$3,375	

8   Here is how you would post the information from the Cash Disbursements Journal:

Rent Expenses

Date	Description	Ref. No.	Debit	Credit	Balance
5/31	Cash Disbursements Journal	Page 3	$1,500		

Accounts Payable

Date	Description	Ref. No.	Debit	Credit	Balance
5/31	Cash Disbursements Journal	Page 3	$3,250		

Credit Card Payable

Date	Description	Ref. No.	Debit	Credit	Balance
5/31	Cash Disbursements Journal	Page 3	$550		

Salaries

Date	Description	Ref. No.	Debit	Credit	Balance
5/31	Cash Disbursements Journal	Page 3	$800		

Cash

Date	Description	Ref. No.	Debit	Credit	Balance
5/31	Cash Disbursements Journal	Page 3		$6,100	

9 Here is how you would post the information from the General Journal:

Sales Return

Date	Description	Ref. No.	Debit	Credit	Balance
5/31	General Journal	Page 5	$25		

Accounts Payable

Date	Description	Ref. No.	Debit	Credit	Balance
5/31	General Journal	Page 5	$550		

Credit Card Payable

Date	Description	Ref. No.	Debit	Credit	Balance
5/31	General Journal	Page 5		$700	

Purchases Return

Date	Description	Ref. No.	Debit	Credit	Balance
5/31	General Journal	Page 5		$550	

Accounts Receivable

Date	Description	Ref. No.	Debit	Credit	Balance
5/31	General Journal	Page 5		$25	

Office Furniture

Date	Description	Ref. No.	Debit	Credit	Balance
5/31	General Journal	Page 5	$700		

Chapter 5

Journaling — The Devil's in the Details

In This Chapter
- Understanding journals
- Following cash
- Monitoring sales
- Tracking purchases

*N*ot every business transaction can be found in the General Ledger. Imagine how many volumes the General Leger would need to be if every single purchase, every single credit for the return of an item, and every other financial activity was individually listed in the General Ledger? For a major corporation this can be thousands or even millions of transactions each month.

To keep the General Ledger more manageable journals are kept for active accounts and only their daily, weekly, or monthly summaries are posted to the General Ledger. In this chapter you'll find the types of accounts for which journals are kept and how entries are made in these journals.

Defining Your Journals

Journals give you a place to look for the details on every transaction in your business. Rather than jumble all the thousands of transactions in the General Ledger (see Chapter 4), which would make it difficult to find anything, bookkeepers set up a series of journals for the most active accounts, such as Cash Receipts, Cash Disbursements, Sales, and Purchases.

Using these journals, the detail can easily be found about specific financial activity and a summary of the day's, week's, or month's activity are posted to the General Ledger so that financial reporting can be done. Think of the journals as a place for the details and the General Ledger as the place you look for the big picture.

When entering a transaction in your books the first place it is entered is the journal for that type of transaction. Journals are kept in chronological order. For example the sales transactions for the day would be entered into the Sales Journal.

Each entry should include information about the date of the transaction, the accounts to which the transaction will be posted, and the location of the source material used for developing the transaction. After posting to the Sales Journal, you would then post the information to the accounts impacted by the transaction. For example, suppose a customer bought an item on store credit. You would post the information from the Sales Journal to the customer's account in addition to the summary that will be posted to the General Ledger.

Tracking Cash

You'll deal with cash transactions many times every day and you certainly want to keep track of every penny that goes in and out of your business. In fact, cash transactions are so numerous that bookkeepers keep two journals — one for incoming cash (Cash Receipts Journal) and one for outgoing cash (Cash Disbursements Journal). That way a business owner can quickly get a summary of how much cash came into the business and how much cash went out of the business in any one day, week, or month.

Tracking the Receipts

The first place you enter cash receipts in your books is the Cash Receipts Journal. The majority of that cash will come from sales, but other possible sources of cash include deposits of capital from the company's owner, customer bill payments, new loan proceeds, and interest from savings accounts.

When you enter the cash in the books you must indicate how it was received and into which account it was credited. For example, when a customer pays a bill the cash would be debited to the Cash account and credited to the Accounts Receivable account. You don't put it into the Sales account, because that account was credited when the Sale was originally completed and the Accounts Receivable account was debited. Now you have to reverse that debit to Accounts Receivable with a credit to indicate that the money is no longer due. In addition, you would need to credit the payment to the customer's individual account as well.

In Figure 5-1, I show you a sample page in a Cash Receipts Journal. Note that there are seven columns of information:

Date: Transaction date

Account Credited: Account that will be credited

PR (post reference): This information is filled in at the end of the month to indicate where in the General Ledger the information is posted. As you post to the General Ledger you indicate the completion of that post in the column so you can be sure you haven't missed anything. At the end of the month when the information is posted the columns will be totaled. You can post just the summary total of the Accounts Receivable, Sales, and Cash accounts and put a check next to the entries that are part of the summary total. Any entries that are not part of the summary total will need to be posted individually to the General Ledger and an indication of where it was posted would be put in the PR column.

General Credit: This column is for transactions that are not tracked in their own column in the journal, since it involves an account that does not frequently involve a cash transaction. In Figure 5-1 you see that Art (one of the owner's) made a cash deposit into the business of $1,500.

Accounts Receivable Credit: All customer payments are credited to this column and will be summarized to the Accounts Receivable account at the end of the month.

Sales Credit: Total cash sales for each day are credited to this column and will be summarized in the Sales account at the end of the month.

Cash Debit: The total of this column will be debited to the Cash account at the end of the month. Remember a debit to the Cash account increases the balance of that account.

Figure 5-1:
This sample page of a Cash Receipts Journal shows you how incoming cash transactions are first entered into the books.

			ABC Candy Shop						
			Cash Receipts Journal						
			July 2007						
Date	Account Credited	PR	General Debit	Accounts Receivable Debit	Sales Debit	Cash Debit
7|1	Sales				300-	300-
7|2	Sales				250-	250-
7|3	CK 125 from P. Smith			200-		200-
7|3	Sales				150-	150-
7|4	Art's Capital		1500-			1500-
7|5	CK 320 – J. Johns			100-		100-
7|5	CK 575 – P. Post			200-		200-
7|5	Sales				200-	200-

If you have another account with frequent cash inflows, you can add a column to track that account just as Accounts Receivable, Sales, and Cash are tracked in Figure 5-1. The big advantage to having columns for active accounts is that you can post a summary entry into the General Ledger at the end of the month, rather than an individual entry for each transaction. It saves a lot of time and minimizes the bits of information that must be posted to the General Ledger.

Q. Post these transactions in June 2007 to the Cash Receipts Journal page below:

June 1	Sales	$200
June 2	Sales	$350
June 3	Check 152 from Jane Doe, a customer	$200
June 3	Sales	$220

A. Here is how the transactions would be posted:

ABC Candy Company Cash Receipts Journal — June 2007

Date	Account Credited	PR	General Credit	Accounts Receivable Credit	Sales Credit	Cash Debit
6/1	Sales				$200	$200
6/2	Sales				$350	$350
6/3	CK 152, J. Doe			$200		$200
6/3	Sales				$220	$220

1. Post these transactions in May 2007 to the Cash Receipts Journal page below:

May 1	Sales	$350
May 2	Sales	$300
May 3	Check 220 from John James, a customer	$250
May 3	Sales	$250
May 4	Check 225 from Art, an owner, for additional capital	$1,000
May 4	Sales	$325

Solve It

ABC Candy Company Cash Receipts Journal — May 2007

Date	Account Credited	PR	General Credit	Accounts Receivable Credit	Sales Credit	Cash Debit

2. Post these transactions in August 2007 to the Cash Receipts Journal page below:

August 1	Sales	$225
August 2	Sales	$125
August 3	Check 256 from Amy Smith, a customer	$150
August 3	Sales	$350
August 4	Cash from sale of unused office furniture	$750
August 4	Sales	$325

Solve It

ABC Candy Company Cash Receipts Journal — August 2007

Date	Account Credited	PR	General Credit	Accounts Receivable Credit	Sales Credit	Cash Debit

Keeping an eye on outgoing cash

Cash sent out of the business is tracked in a similar way to Cash Receipts using a Cash Disbursements Journal. In this journal, you would track bills you pay, salaries, rent and any other use of business cash. In this case all the accounts involved are debited and the Cash account is credited. A credit to the Cash account reduces the amount of cash you have available.

In Figure 5-2, you will see that some of the columns for the Cash Disbursement Journal look similar — the Date, Account Debited, PR and General Debit (for miscellaneous debits) are the first four columns. You add Accounts Payable debit (for bills paid) and Salaries debit (for cash used to pay employees). The final column is for the Cash Credit. You can add more columns for accounts that experience frequent transactions during the month.

Figure 5-2:
This sample page of a Cash Disbursements Journal shows you how outgoing cash transactions are first entered into the books.

Date	Account Debited	PR	General Debit	Accounts Receivable Debit	Sales Debit	Cash Debit
7 1	Sales		1500 –			1500 –
7 3	Sales			1500 –		1500 –
7 4	Acct. Payable – Joe's			500 –		500 –
7 10	Acct. Payable – Ruth's				800 –	800 –
7 20	Salaries			425 –		425 –

3. Post these transactions in May 2007 to the Cash Disbursements Journal page below:

May 1	Rent	$1,500
May 2	Accounts Payable, Joe's Supplies	$2,000
May 3	Accounts Payable, Ruth's Sweets	$575
May 5	Salaries	$800
May 4	Credit Card Payment	$1,000

Solve It

ABC Candy Company Cash Disbursements Journal — May 2007						
Date	Account Debited	PR	General Debit	Accounts Payable Debit	Salaries Debit	Cash Credit

4. Post these transactions in August 2007 to the Cash Disbursements Journal page below:

August 1	Rent	$1,500
August 2	Accounts Payable, Joe's Supplies	$1,200
August 3	Accounts Payable, Ruth's Sweets	$325
August 5	Salaries	$800
August 5	Credit Card Payment	$250
August 4	Art, an owner, pays himself back for cash previous deposited in the business	$1,000

Solve It

ABC Candy Company Cash Disbursements Journal — August 2007						
Date	Account Debited	PR	General Debit	Accounts Payable Debit	Salaries Debit	Cash Credit

Managing Sales

If your business permits customers to buy on store credit, then not all sales involve the use of cash. Non-cash sales are tracked in a Sales Journal. When you make an entry in the Sales Journal you credit sales, but you also must remember to update the customer's individual record so that you can bill the customer at the end of the month.

The most common columns you'll find in a Sales Journal include Date, Customer Account Debited, PR, Invoice Number, Accounts Receivable Debit, and Sales Credit. Note that in this journal you track both the customer name and the invoice, so that if the customer has a question when the bill comes in, you will have enough detail in the Sales Journal to send out a copy of the transaction.

The Sales journal allows the bookkeeper to project future cash inflows based on outstanding customer accounts. The owner can use the information to project possible cash shortage or plan for extra cash that can be used to grow the business when the money comes in.

5. Post these transactions in July 2007 to the Sales Journal page below:

July 1	Sale to Susan Smith, Inv. #245	$500
July 2	Sale to Charlie's Café, Inv. #246	$1,200
July 3	Sale to Peter Perry, Inv. #247	$325
July 5	Sale to Jim Jones, Inv. #249	$125
July 4	Sale to Peter's Palace, Inv. #248	$2,500

Solve It

ABC Candy Company Sales Journal — July 2007

Date	Customer Account Credited	PR	Invoice Number	Accounts Receivable Debit	Sales Credit

6. Post these transactions in August 2007 to the Sales Journal page below:

August 1	Sale to Susan Smith, Inv. #301	$150
August 2	Sale to Charlie's Café, Inv. #302	$750
August 3	Sale to Peter Perry, Inv. #303	$175
August 5	Sale to Jim Jones, Inv. #304	$95
August 5	Sale to Peter's Palace, Inv. #305	$1,500

Solve It

ABC Candy Company Sales Journal — August 2007					
Date	Customer Account Credited	PR	Invoice Number	Accounts Receivable Debit	Sales Credit

Watching Purchases

A common way for business people to obligate future cash purchases, without actually laying out any cash, is through purchase orders for supplies and other business needs. Bookkeepers track these noncash obligations in the Purchases Journal. Using the Purchases Journal, the bookkeeper can quickly know the level of cash that will be needed to pay bills during the next month.

Common columns in the Purchases Journal include the date, Vendor Account Credited (where you indicate the company from where the items were purchased), PR, Invoice Number, Purchases Debit (expenses from Purchases), and Accounts Payable credit. When the Accounts Payable account is credited, that means the account increases in value and additional money will be owed in the future.

Invoice numbers will not be consecutive for purchases because the number is supplied by the company from which you ordered. You enter the transaction in the Purchases account when you receive the invoice for the goods ordered. Payment of the invoice will be made after you receive approval from the department that ordered the goods. You should check for that approval before paying an invoice, in case there are any problems with the delivery.

7. Post these transactions in July 2007 to the Purchases Journal page below:

July 1	Supplies from Ruth's Sweets, Inv. #1345	$500
July 2	Boxes from Henry's Packing Supplies, Inv. #275	$1,500
July 3	Supplies from Deb's Paper Goods, Inv. #356	$575
July 5	Food from Karen's Grocery, Inv. #1234	$125

Solve It

ABC Candy Company Purchases Journal — July 2007					
Date	*Vendor Account Credited*	*PR*	*Invoice Number*	*Purchases Debit*	*Accounts Payable Credit*

8. Post these transactions in August 2007 to the Purchases Journal page below:

August 1	Supplies from Ruth's Sweets, Inv. #1345	$575
August 2	Food from Karen's Grocery, Inv. #1234	$315
August 3	Boxes from Henry's Packing Supplies, Inv. #275	$1,250
August 5	Supplies from Deb's Paper Goods, Inv. #356	$1,200

Solve It

ADC Candy Company Purchases Journal — August 2007					
Date	*Vendor Account Credited*	*PR*	*Invoice Number*	*Purchases Debit*	*Accounts Payable Credit*

Dealing with Miscellaneous Transactions

Not all of your transactions will fit neatly into one of these four main journals. If you have frequent transactions and you want to establish another journal, you can always create one developing the columns that can track the needed information. Otherwise, you can put miscellaneous transactions in a General Journal and post them to the General Ledger at the end of the month.

Common columns in a General Journal include the Date, Account, PR, General Debit (for most debits), and General Credit (for most credits). You will also find that these miscellaneous transactions usually impact Accounts Payable or Accounts Receivable accounts. It's good to add a column for each of those accounts.

The primary description of the transaction will be in the second column, called "Account." In this column you will probably need more detail about the transaction than with other journals because you will be posting so many different types of transactions impacting various accounts. In Figure 5-3, I show you a sample page from a General Journal.

Note that in Figure 5-3, a Sales Return is entered in the General Debit column and will be posted to the Sales Return account in the General Ledger, while the credit is posted in the Accounts Receivable Credit column because a returned item means the amount due from the customer is reduced. You will also need to use the information in the column to indicate details about whose account should be credited.

Figure 5-3:
This sample page of a General Journal shows you how miscellaneous transactions are first entered into the books.

ABC Candy Shop
General Journal
May 2007

Date	Account	PR	General Debit	General Credit	Accounts Payable Debit	Accounts Receivable
5 6	Sales Return		25 —			25 —
	S. Smith					
	Credit Memo 134					
5 15	Henry's Packing			450 —	450 —	
	Purchase Return					
	Debit Memo 1235					
5 20	Deb's Paper Goods			100 —	100 —	
	Purchase Return					
	Debit Memo 256					
5 25	Office Furniture		700 —	700 —		
	(Inv. 1236)					
	Credit Card Payable					

The Purchase Return to Henry's Packing shows debit memo detail. The Purchase Return account will be credited and the Accounts Payable will be debited. The business owes less money to Henry's Packing. The same is true for the purchase return transaction and debit memo from Deb's Paper Goods.

The final transaction on that journal page is the purchase of office furniture with a credit card. In this case both the debit and credit are put in the general columns because neither the Accounts Payable nor the Accounts Receivable accounts will be impacted by that transaction.

9. Post these transactions in May 2007 to the General Journal page below:

May 1	Sales Return from Henry Hope, Credit Memo #346	$75
May 2	Sales Return from Sally Smith, Credit Memo #347	$120
May 3	Purchase Return to Henry's Packing, Debit Memo #1236	$525
May 5	Purchase of Office Supplies by Credit Card, Inv. #378	$575

Solve It

ABC Candy Company General Journal — May 2007

Date	Account	PR	General Debit	General Credit	Accounts Payable Debit	Accounts Receivable Credit

10. Post these transactions in August 2007 to the General Journal page below:

August 1	Sales Return from Pam Smith, Credit Memo #349	$35
August 2	Sales Return from Gary Green, Credit Memo #350	$25
August 3	Office Supplies purchase on credit card, invoice #678	$425
August 5	Purchase Return to Ruth's Sweets, Debit Memo #789	$125

Solve It

ABC Candy Company General Journal — August 2007

Date	Account	PR	General Debit	General Credit	Accounts Payable Debit	Accounts Receivable Credit

Answers to Problems on Journaling — The Devil's in the Details

1 Here are the posts to the Cash Receipts Journal:

ABC Candy Company Cash Receipts Journal — May 2007

Date	Account Credited	PR	General Credit	Accounts Receivable Credit	Sales Credit	Cash Debit
5/1	Sales				$350	$350
5/2	Sales				$300	$300
5/3	CK 220 from J. James			$250		$250
5/3	Sales				$250	$250
5/4	Art's Capital		$1,000			$1,000
5/4	Sales				$325	$325

2 Here are the posts to the Cash Receipts Journal:

ABC Candy Company Cash Receipts Journal — August 2007

Date	Account Credited	PR	General Credit	Accounts Receivable Credit	Sales Credit	Cash Debit
8/1	Sales				$225	$225
8/2	Sales				$125	$125
8/3	CK 256 from A. Smith			$150		$150
8/3	Sales				$350	$350
8/4	Office Furniture		$750			$750
8/4	Sales				$325	$325

3 Here are the posts to the Cash Disbursements Journal:

ABC Candy Company Cash Disbursements Journal — May 2007

Date	Account Credited	PR	General Credit	Accounts Receivable Credit	Sales Credit	Cash Debit
5/1	Rent		$1,500			$1,500
5/2	Joe's Supplies			$2,000		$2,000
5/3	Ruth's Supplies			$575		$575
5/4	Credit Card Payment		$1,000			$1,000
5/5	Salaries				$800	$800

Note that I reordered the transactions so they would be in chronological order. All journal entries should be in chronological order.

4 Here are the posts to the Cash Disbursements Journal:

ABC Candy Company Cash Disbursement Journal — August 2007

Date	Account Debited	PR	General Debit	Accounts Payable Debit	Salaries Debit	Cash Credit
8/1	Rent		$1,500			$1,500
8/2	Joe's Supplies			$1,200		$1,200
8/3	Ruth's Sweets			$325		$325
8/4	Art's Drawing		$1,000			$1,000
8/5	Salaries				$800	$800
8/5	Credit Card Payment			$250		$250

5 Here are the posts to the Sales Journal:

ABC Candy Company Sales Journal — July 2007

Date	Customer Account Credited	PR	Invoice Number	Accounts Receivable Debit	Sales Credit
7/1	Susan Smith		245	$500	$500
7/2	Charlie's Café		246	$1,200	$1,200
7/3	Peter Perry		247	$325	$325
7/4	Peter's Palace		248	$2,500	$2,500
7/5	Jim Jones		249	$125	$125

6 Here are the posts to the Sales Journal:

ABC Candy Company Sales Journal — August 2007

Date	Customer Account Credited	PR	Invoice Number	Accounts Receivable Debit	Sales Credit
8/1	Susan Smith		301	$150	$150
8/2	Charlie's Café		302	$750	$750
8/3	Peter Perry		303	$175	$175
8/5	Jim Jones		304	$95	$95
8/5	Peter's Palace		305	$1,500	$1,500

7 Here are the posts to the Purchases Journal:

ABC Candy Company Purchases Journal — July 2007

Date	Vendor Account Credited	PR	Invoice Number	Purchases Debit	Accounts Payable Credit
7/1	Ruth's Sweets		1,345	$500	$500
7/2	Henry's Packing Supplies		275	$1,500	$1,500
7/3	Deb's Paper Goods		356	$575	$575
7/5	Karen's Grocery		1,234	$125	$125

8 Here are the posts to the Purchases Journal:

ABC Candy Company Purchases Journal — August 2007

Date	Vendor Account Credited	PR	Invoice Number	Purchases Debit	Accounts Payable Credit
8/1	Ruth's Sweets		1,345	$575	$575
8/2	Karen's Grocery		1,234	$315	$315
8/3	Henry's Packing Supplies		275	$1,250	$1,250
8/5	Deb's Paper Goods		356	$1,200	$1,200

9 Here are the posts to the General Journal:

ABC Candy Company General Journal — May 2007

Date	Account	PR	General Debit	General Credit	Accounts Payable Debit	Accounts Receivable Credit
5/1	Sales Return, Henry Hope, Credit Memo #346		$75			$75
5/2	Sales Return, Sally Smith, Credit Memo #347		$120			$120
5/3	Purchase Return, Henry's Packing, Debit Memo 1236			$525	$525	
5/5	Office Supplies purchase by credit card, Inv. #378		$575	$575		

10 Here are the posts to the General Journal:

ABC Candy Company General Journal — August 2007

Date	Account	PR	General Debit	General Credit	Accounts Payable Debit	Accounts Receivable Credit
8/1	Sales Return, Pam Smith, Credit Memo #349		$35			$35
8/2	Sales Return, Gary Green, Credit Memo #350		$25			$25
8/3	Office Supplies, purchase on credit card invoice #678		$425	$425		
8/5	Purchase Return, Ruth's Sweets Debit Memo #789			$125	$125	

Chapter 6

Designing Controls for Your Books, Your Records, and Your Money

*B*efore even opening the door of your business, establishing strong internal processes and controls for business operations is crucial. How employees will handle and monitor cash taken in or paid out, can make or break a business.

In this chapter, you will review the key concepts of how to set up cash handling procedures. You will find ideas about how to design filing systems to be sure you keep all the proper records. You'll also discover how to develop internal control procedures for your company's assets.

Getting a Handle on Cash

Cash flows through you business in four key ways:

✔ Deposits into and payments out of your checking accounts

✔ Deposits to and withdrawals from your savings accounts

✔ Petty cash availability in certain key locations where cash payments may be required

✔ Cash register transactions

You must be able to track when cash comes in and when cash goes out at any of the four locations. Without proper handling, you'll find cash has a way to slip through the cracks and out of your business.

Finding the right bank and controlling banking transactions

Your main tools for tracking the use of your cash are the bank or banks you choose for your accounts. You want a bank that is open the hours you need it and that has a way to deposit funds 24 hours a day, You also want a bank located near your business, so it will be convenient for you and your employees to conduct business.

In addition to location and times of operation, you want a bank that will offer you all the services you need. Check carefully to find out how much the bank charges for each of the services you expect to need. You will find service charges vary greatly among banks and you can save a lot of money if you shop carefully for a bank. Some banks charge for every transaction done with a teller; others charge for transaction at the automatic teller machine (ATM). Some charge if you want copies of your checks. Others charge to get your checks printed, while some will print checks for free. Write down the services that are important to your business and find out what those services will cost at each of the banks you are considering.

Picking Checks

The check style you choose can be critical to managing dispersal of funds. First you need to think about how you will disperse checks. You can do it by handwriting each check or you can print your checks by computer. You will need different checks depending on how you plan to prepare your checks.

If you plan to do them by writing them out manually, then you will need to order voucher checks. Voucher checks usually are printed three to a page and put into a binder. When the check is written, the voucher to the left is completed to list the date, who the check was written to, and the reason for the check. On the right of the voucher you keep a running total of your checking account balance.

Each check and voucher is numbered to match and if a voucher or check is missing, you must find out why and how the check was used. It could be a sign of misuse of company funds. When someone makes a mistake in writing out, a check the voided check and voucher should be left in the checkbook, so you can account for all numbered checks.

If you plan to print your checks as needed by computer, then you would order checks based on the computerized bookkeeping system you use.

These checks are printed with the top third of the page the actual check to be cashed. The middle third is where detail is printed for the customer about the dispersal, such as payment of a particular invoice or contract. The bottom third would have all the detail you need to track the use of the check in your own accounting system. Note that each of the three sections has a matching number in the upper-left corner. Your computerized print checks will be numbered and if you find a missing number that could be the sign of a check not used appropriately. You will need to find out how the missing check was used. Any checks on which a mistake was made should be saved and voided, so you can keep track of all numbered checks.

Signing checks

In addition to setting up a procedure for controlling the preparation of checks, you also need to set up controls about who can sign checks and let the bank know the controls you have in place. For example, you may decide that certain people in the company are authorized to sign checks of $1,000 or less and others can sign checks between $1,000 and $10,000. You may want to require two signatures on all checks over $10,000.

Your bank can help you establish check-signing authority and will have forms you'll need to complete to designate authorized employees. Each authorized employee will need to sign the form, so that the bank has a copy of the signature on file in case a question about a check arises.

Handling deposits

Another key point of entry, depositing of funds, must also be carefully monitored and recorded. First, you should tell whoever opens the mail to immediately stamp "for deposit only" on the back of any check received, so you don't risk the check being used fraudulently. Your best bet is to have a stamp made up that says "For deposit only" as well as your bank account number. That way you know all checks will be deposited in the right account. Some companies where a lot of checks come by mail require that two people be involved in the opening of the mail to avoid any misappropriation of funds.

When all checks are ready for deposit, the person preparing the deposit should list the number of all checks being deposited, the company or individual that sent the check, and the amount of the check. Then all checks should be copied, so you have a record of the checks in case there is an error at the bank or a question about the check. After the deposit is completed a receipt for the deposit, a copy of the list of checks, and all the photocopied checks should be attached together and filed in your daily bank folder. I talk more about "Organizing Your Record Keeping" below.

Q. When trying to find the right bank, what should you look for?

a. How close the bank is to your business

b. The hours of operation

c. The cost of services

d. All of the above

A. The answer would be **d.** All three issues are key to finding the right bank.

---

1. When choosing a check design for a business account, what style of check should you use if you plan to prepare your checks manually?

a. Voucher

b. Notebook

c. Loose-leaf

d. Pad

Solve It

2. If you plan to print out your checks by computer, what are the key things you must consider?

a. A check style that is compatible with your computer software.

b. A check system that will allow you to print the backup detail for both you and your customer.

c. A check style that prints the corresponding number for the check on the backup detail.

d. All of the above.

Solve It

3. What should you have your staff do when they find a check that has come in the mail?

    a. Give it immediately to the bookkeeper.

    b. Stamp it "for deposit only."

    c. Give it to their manager.

    d. Keep it for themselves as an extra bonus.

Solve It

4. Who should you allow to sign your business checks?

    a. Set up a procedure for check authorization.

    b. Work with the bank to be sure authorized signatures are on file.

    c. Let anyone in accounting sign the checks.

    d. Both a and b.

Solve It

Savings accounts

If you do have extra cash that won't be needed for the daily operations of the business, you probably will want to deposit this cash in an interest bearing account. You can set up a transfer between the checking and savings accounts, but you should be very careful about who is authorized to access that transfer capability. For many small businesses, only the owner or the owner and his partners will have access to transfer money between checking and savings accounts. In a larger corporation, the transfer rights may be given to the chief financial officer and the comptroller.

Petty cash accounts

Many businesses find they have a need for small amounts of cash for unexpected needs during the week. For example, if a package arrives with postage due, the person at the reception desk may need a couple dollars for the postal delivery person. Employees may have a rush need for office supplies to finish up a project and draw from petty cash to run to a local store rather than wait for the official office supply order.

Whatever the reason you can set up petty cash boxes that are handled by certain trusted staff, such as the office manager. You may designate that they keep $50 to $100 on hand for office cash emergencies. Prepare a form that needs to be completed whenever cash is used. This form should include the name of the person who gets the cash and the purpose for the cash. When a person handling petty cash needs more cash, they must first account for how the cash they had was used.

Cash Registers

If you are running or working for a retail business, most of your cash will come into the business at your point of sale — the cash register. You need tight controls to be sure that cash makes it into the business and not into the pockets of people working the registers. Since you should have them prove out their cash each night, cashiers get more creative than just pocketing cash. There are three ways cashiers can pocket cash without coming up short at the end of the day:

- ✔ **Don't record the sale and pocket the cash:** Make sure your cash register transactions match your sales receipts.

- ✔ **Don't provide a sales receipt and pocket the cash:** To avoid this make sure you post that a receipt is needed for all returns and exchanges. Customers will help you make sure a receipt is prepared for all sales.

- ✔ **Prepare a false credit voucher and keep the cash:** Establish procedures that require a manager's approval for all cash returned.

Whenever cash is involved, it gives employees an enticement that you must control. Businesses put up barriers to make it difficult for employees to pocket cash, if they are in cash handling positions. As the bookkeeper it is your responsibility to be involved in the design of sales receipts and cash vouchers and to be sure these vouchers are being used according to company policy.

Q. Who should control deposits into and withdrawals out of a savings account?

a. Owners or partners

b. Chief financial officer and comptroller

c. Any manager

d. Only a and b

A. If you are working for a small company, the deposit of money into and withdrawals out of a savings account will most likely be handled by the owner or partners. In a large corporation, the chief financial officer and comptroller, or someone they specifically designate, will likely be responsible for major disbursements from a savings account.

5. What should you set up for small cash needs in the day to day operation of your business?

   a. Bank account with ATM card for employees

   b. Petty cash box

   c. A cookie jar with cash

   d. Require employees to contact the book-keeper when cash is needed

Solve It

6. Employees at cash registers sometimes keep the cash for themselves. What is not a likely way that cashiers may try to pocket cash?

   a. Don't record the sale and pocket the cash.

   b. Don't give a sales receipt and keep the cash.

   c. Prepare a false credit voucher and keep the cash.

   d. Just take cash out of the register and put it in their pocket.

Solve It

7. If you want to be sure your cashiers don't prepare a false credit voucher and just pocket the cash for themselves, what should you do?

   a. Don't allow the cashiers to handle credit vouchers.

   b. Make sure that all cashiers ask another cashier to witness the transaction.

   c. Don't worry about it, it doesn't happen often.

   d. Require that a manager review and sign off on all credit vouchers.

Solve It

Organizing Your Record Keeping

Everything you do in your business is going to generate paperwork that you may or may not want to keep. You need to decide what to keep, and what you do keep you need to organize so you can access quickly when you need it. If you computerize your accounting you may not need to keep as much paper, but you still want a paper trail in case something happens to your computer records or you need the backup information for a transaction that is questioned at a later date.

Obviously, file cabinets are where you'll store most of your records for the current year and the prior year. Older files you may store in boxes in a warehouse or storeroom if you don't have room in your file cabinets. How you set up the files can be critical to your ability to find something when you need it. Many bookkeepers use four different methods to store accounting information:

✔ **File folders:** these are used for filing invoice, payment, and contract information about vendors; information about individual employees, such as payroll related forms and data; and information about individual customer accounts.

✔ **Three-ring binders:** Your Chart of Accounts (see Chapter 3), General Ledger (see Chapter 4), and Journals (see Chapter 5) are usually kept in three-ring binders. Even if you do use a computerized accounting system, it's a good idea to keep a copy of this for the month most recently closed and the current month in hard copy in case your computer system goes down and you need to quickly check information.

✔ **Expandable files:** These types of files are good for managing outstanding bills and vendor activity. You can get alphabetical expandable files for managing pending vendor invoices and purchase orders. You can use 30-day and 12-month expandable files for managing outstanding bills. As bills come in you can place them in the 12-month file for the month they are due. Then move the current month's bills to the 30-day file by the day they are due. You may be able to avoid using these files if you are using a computerized bookkeeping system and set up the bill pay reminder system in your accounting program.

✔ **Media for storing backup computer data:** If you are keeping the books on computer, be certain you make at least one backup copy of all your data daily and store it in a safe place — a place where the data won't be destroyed if there is a fire. A good alternative could be a small fire safe if your business does not have a built-in safe.

You'll find it doesn't take long to build up lots of paper and not have room to store it all. Luckily not everything has to be kept forever. Generally anything related to tax returns has to be kept for at least three years, but once you're past three years the IRS can't audit you unless it suspects fraud. So you can get rid of most of your paperwork once it is four years old.

Some exceptions include employees. Those records you must keep until the employee has left the employment of the company for at least three years. The statute of limitations for most actions that can be filed by an ex-employee is three years after they left.

In the fourth year, you will be able to get rid of most of your paperwork, but you may want to keep certain sensitive data longer. Any information about assets that are still held by the company should be kept. You also should keep any information about pending legal issues. Check with your attorney and your accountant before destroying old paperwork and be certain you are not tossing something that could be needed.

EXAMPLE

Q. Where is the best place to store information about vendor transactions?

  a. In file folders

  b. In expandable folders

  c. In three-ring binders

  d. No need to keep the information

A. The answer is **a.** While you will keep information about bills due in expandable folders initially before the bill is paid, for long-term storage after payment of the bill you should make up a file folder for each vendor.

8. Where would you keep a paper copy of your General Ledger?

  a. In file folders

  b. In expandable folders

  c. In three-ring binders

  d. No need to keep the information

Solve It

9. Where would you put a copy of a bill not yet paid?

  a. In file folders

  b. In expandable folders

  c. In three-ring binders

  d. No need to keep the information

Solve It

10. Where would you file information about an employee's payroll history?

  a. In file folders

  b. In expandable folders

  c. In three-ring binders

  d. No need to keep the information

Solve It

Protecting Your Business from Theft and Fraud

Every business owner faces the possibility of theft or fraud. Too often business owners find out about an employee pocketing some assets when it's too late to do anything about it. Even the most loyal employee can be driven to steal if their personal financial pressures become too great. There are four basic types of financial fraud a business owner may face:

- ✔ **Embezzlement:** This involves the theft of funds by a person who actually has control of the funds, such as a bookkeeper or comptroller.

- ✔ **Internal theft:** This involves the theft of company assets by employees, such as office supplies or merchandise on store shelves.

- ✔ **Payoffs and kickbacks:** This involves the acceptance of payments by vendors for sending business their way.

- ✔ **Skimming:** This involves pocketing some of the company's sales receipts and not recording the revenue on the books.

Your best defense against theft and fraud is to put up barriers to discourage it. You do this by dividing staff responsibilities to reduce the possibility and opportunity for theft and fraud. Here are some key tips for controlling your cash and minimizing theft and fraud:

- ✔ **Separate cash handlers:** Be sure that the person who accepts the cash is not the same person who records the transaction in the books.

- ✔ **Separate authorization responsibilities:** Be sure that the person who authorizes a check is not the same as the person who prepares the check. If possible a third person should be the one to sign the checks. That way three people would have to collude to steal money using a company check.

- ✔ **Separate bookkeeping functions:** Don't put too much authority or trust in one person (unless that person is the business owner).

- ✔ **Separate operational responsibility:** Be sure you have one person who accepts the cash transactions and a second person who enters those transactions in the books. For example the person who handles the cash register should not be the one who makes the bank deposit.

- ✔ **Separate financial reporting:** Be sure that the person who prepares your financial reports is not the same person who is responsible for entering the data day to day in your books. Often an outside accountant is responsible for using the data entered to prepare the financial reports if a business does not have an accountant on staff.

Q. If an employee who keeps the books, finds a way to fudge the numbers and take some of the business's cash for himself, this is called

a. Embezzlement

b. Internal theft

c. Kickback

d. Skimming

A. The answer is **a,** embezzlement. When money is stolen by someone responsible for the books it is considered embezzlement.

11. If a purchaser for the company works a deal to get paid $1,000 under the table if he gets his company to agree to a contract by a certain vendor, this is called

   a. Embezzlement

   b. Internal theft

   c. Kickback

   d. Skimming

Solve It

12. If a cashier fails to enter a transaction and give the customer a sales receipt, but instead pockets the cash, this is called

   a. Embezzlement

   b. Internal theft

   c. Kickback

   d. Skimming

Solve It

13. When setting up the accounting department, which types of tasks require separation of duties?

   a. The person who accepts the cash should not enter the transaction in the books.

   b. The person who enters the data in the books on a daily basis should not prepare the financial statements.

   c. The person who prepares the checks should not have the authority to sign the checks.

   d. All of the above.

Solve It

Taking Out a Bond

Whenever you have employees who you expect to handle a lot of cash, you should consider insuring your business against possible theft. This type of insurance is called fidelity bonds, which are commonly included as part of an overall insurance package.

If you do carry this type of insurance and an employee steals money, you are covered for the loss of those funds. You also have coverage if an employee's act causes a loss to a client of your business. For more information on fidelity bonds talk with your business insurance agent.

Answers to Problems on Designing Controls for Your Books, Your Records, and Your Money

1 **A:** Voucher. The voucher portion of the checkbook is used to control the use of checks and keep detail about how the check is used.

2 **D:** All of the above.

3 **B:** Stamp it "for deposit only."

4 **D:** Both A and B.

5 **B:** Petty Cash Box

6 **D:** Just take cash out of the register and put it in his pocket. Since the cashier must prove out the register at night, he is not likely to just pocket cash. He is more likely to use one of the other options mentioned in the question to try to hide his theft.

7 **D:** The best way to control credit vouchers is to require that a manager review and approve the credit voucher before cash is given to a customer.

8 **C:** In three-ring binders

9 **B:** Expandable. When you first get a bill you will most likely put it in the 12-month expandable folder in the section for the month the bill is due. After the bill is paid you would then put it in the file folder for the vendor.

10 **A:** In file folders. You should have a file folder set up for each employee in which you store all federal, state, and local tax forms completed by the employee; all benefit forms; and any other information related to payroll items.

11 **A:** Embezzlement.

12 **D:** Skimming. Embezzlement would be the taking of cash by someone who controls the books and internal theft is the theft of company assets.

13 **D:** All of the above.

Part III

Tracking Day-to-Day Business Operations with Your Books

The 5th Wave   By Rich Tennant

"If we cut our dividend, reduce inventory and time travel to the 13th century, we should be able to last another year."

In this part . . .

Do you want to know every single financial transaction that happens in your business each and every day? You should. That's the only way you'll be able to put all the pieces together and see how well your business is doing financially.

I show you how to track your day-to-day business operations by recording sales and purchases, as well as any discounts and returns. You'll also need to pay your employees, so I show you the basics of setting up and managing employee payroll and all the government paperwork you must do once you hire employees.

Chapter 7

Purchasing Goods and Tracking Your Purchases

In This Chapter

▶ Controlling inventory

▶ Paying for what you get

*E*very business must have something to sell. Whether selling products or services, you do spend money on items that will later be sold, which becomes inventory until sold. You also need supplies to run the business.

This chapter reviews how to track your purchases, manage inventory, and pay for the items bought. You'll practice how to value your inventory and pay the bills.

Detailing and Managing Your Inventory

Bookkeepers track their inventory in two different accounts — Purchases and Inventory. When you initially buy goods to sell, those transactions are tracked in the Purchases account, which is an expense account and shown on the Income Statement (see Chapter 16 for more information on the Income Statement). When you prepare your financial reports at the end of the month, any goods still on the shelves are then tracked in an asset account called Inventory, which is shown on the Balance Sheet (see Chapter 15 for more information on the Balance Sheet).

When tracking that inventory, companies do so in two different ways — periodic inventory and perpetual inventory:

✔ **Periodic inventory:** When goods on hand are tracked using a periodic inventory system, a physical count is conducted of the goods in the store as well as in the ware-house. This count can be done on a daily, monthly, quarterly, or yearly basis. In an active retail environment, store counts often are done daily. You've probably seen signs on store windows indicating that the store is closed for an entire day to count inventory. That usually happens at the end of the year as a company prepares its financial statements or in the process of a company audit.

✔ **Perpetual inventory:** When goods on hand are tracked as they are sold, that's called a perpetual inventory system. This type of system must be done using a computer software program that is integrated with the accounting system. You'll see this today in many major retail stores where bar codes are used and the actual item purchased shows on your receipt. Inventory counts are adjusted automatically. Even when this type of system is used a physical count of inventory will be done periodically to verify that the inventory numbers in the computerized database actually match what's on the shelf and in the warehouse. Some goods are lost to theft; others are lost to damage. The only way the computer system can be adjusted to actual numbers on hand is through a physical count.

Q. If you purchase goods with cash and plan to sell them to customers, which accounts would be impacted by that transaction?

a. Purchases and Cash

b. Purchases and Accounts Payable

c. Inventory and Cash

d. Inventory and Accounts Payable

A. This answer would be **a,** Purchases and Cash. You would enter a debit to the Purchases account, which would increase the balance in the account and show the additional expense. You would enter a credit to the Cash account, which would decrease the balance in that account.

---

1. If you keep track of the amount of inventory you have on hand by counting how much product is on your store shelves and in your warehouse, this is called

a. A perpetual inventory system

b. A periodic inventory system

c. A physical inventory system

d. A counting inventory system

Solve It

2. If your inventory is counted each time you ring up a sale on your register, this is called

a. A perpetual inventory system

b. A periodic inventory system

c. A physical inventory system

d. A counting inventory system

Solve It

Determining inventory value

When you first enter a purchase in the books, you enter its value based on the cost that you paid for those goods. But, the way you track the value of that inventory is often not the same as the actual cost. For example, a hardware store that buys and sells hammers can't possibly keep track of how much it paid for each individual hammer on the shelf. One week when an order comes in the price from the manufacturer may be $5 for the hammer and the next week it may be $5.50. It would be a nightmare for the store owner to keep track of the price on each hammer and then calculate exactly how much profit was made on each hammer.

Instead of trying to track each individual item, bookkeepers use various methods for valuing inventory. Your company must choose one method and follow that method all the time. If the company decides to change its inventory valuation method, than it must file forms with the IRS. The value of inventory sold can impact how much profit a company will make. Let's look at how that happens.

The four most common types of inventory valuing methods include

- ✔ **LIFO (Last In, First Out):** With this method of valuing inventory, a store owner assumes that the last product put on the shelf is the first product sold when he's calculating the value of his inventory for the books and his financial report. LIFO is most often used by a business that does not have to worry about spoilage. For example a hardware store that receives new hammers is not likely to carefully empty the shelves, put the newest hammers at the back of the shelf and then put the oldest hammers in the front. Instead, when a new shipment arrives the newest hammers will be put out front, so they'll be sold first. The actual price he sells his hammers to customers will be the same no matter when he put them on the shelves.

- ✔ **FIFO (First In, First Out):** With this method of valuing inventory, a store owner assumes that the first in (oldest item) is the first one sold when he's calculating the value of his inventory for the books and his financial records. Food stores commonly use this system because they must worry about spoilage. When you go to the store, you know that you will always find the oldest milk (the milk that will expire first) at the front of the shelf and the newest milk (the milk with a longer time until expiration) will be in the back. That store is using a first in, first out method of counting inventory — trying to get the product that came in first to sell first.

- ✔ **Averaging:** With this method of inventory, a company doesn't worry about what came in first or last. Instead it averages the cost of inventory when calculating inventory value.

- ✔ **Specific identification:** With this method of inventory, the store owner does keep track of how much he paid for each individual item. This type of inventory method is only used when big ticket items are sold. For example, a car dealer will keep track of how much he paid for each car and for how much each car sold.

3. If you work in a grocery store and carefully place the newest loaves of bread in the back of the shelf and bring the older loaves of bread to the front of the shelf, what type of inventory system does your store probably use?

a. FIFO

b. LIFO

c. Averaging

d. Specific Identification

Solve It

4. If you work at a car dealership and you must track the sale of a car using the original invoice price, what type of inventory system does your dealership probably use?

a. FIFO

b. LIFO

c. Averaging

d. Specific Identification

Solve It

Calculating the value of ending inventory and cost of goods sold is different with each method. I will give you an example of how to do the calculations for averaging, LIFO, and FIFO and then let you try to calculate a problem on your own.

A hardware store owner purchased hammers several times during the month of April. (He doesn't have a warehouse, so all new goods purchased are put on the store shelves.):

Date	Quantity	Per Hammer Price
April 1	150	$5.00
April 10	150	$7.50
April 20	200	$8.00

He started the month with 50 hammers worth $250. At the end of the month, when he counts what is left on the shelf, he has 75 units left. What is the value of his ending inventory and what was the cost of goods sold?

To calculate inventory value you start with the number of inventory at the beginning of the month. Then add the purchases made during the month. That total will give you the number of goods you had available for sale. Then you subtract the amount of inventory left on the shelf. The inventory left on the shelf would be the ending inventory and the difference between inventory available for sale and ending inventory would be the cost of goods sold. The ending inventory would be the value that you would put in the asset account Inventory shown on the Balance Sheet and the cost of goods shown would be an expense on the Income Statement.

Here is how you would calculate the cost of goods sold and ending inventory using the Averaging method:

Beginning Inventory	50	$250.00
Purchases	150 @ $5.00	$750.00
	150 @ $7.50	$1,125.00
	200 @ $8.00	$1,600.00
Total Goods Available for Sale		$3,725.00
Average Cost per Unit	($3,725/550)	$6.77
Ending Inventory	(75 × $6.77)	$507.75
Cost of Goods Sold	(550–75 = 475 goods sold × $6.77)	$3,215.75

---

5. Harry's Hardware started the month with 25 wrenches on the shelf with an average per unit value of $3.25. During the month he made these additional purchases:

April 1	100 wrenches @ $3.50
April 10	100 wrenches @ $3.75
April 20	150 wrenches @ $4.00

At the end of the month he had 100 wrenches on the shelf. Calculate the value of the ending inventory and the cost of goods sold using the Averaging method.

Solve It

Using the same purchase information for the hammers shown in the example above, how would you calculate the value of the ending inventory and cost of goods sold using the FIFO inventory method? Beginning inventory of 50 hammers purchased at $5 each, ending inventory of 75 hammers. Additional purchases were

Date	Quantity	Per Hammer Price
April 1	150	$5.00
April 10	150	$7.50
April 20	200	$8.00

Since FIFO is first in, first out, you would start the calculation with the beginning inventory of 50 hammers at $5 and assume those were sold first.

Beginning Inventory	50 @ $5.00	$250.00
Next in: April 1	150 @ $5.00	$750.00
Next in: April 10	150 @ $7.50	$1,125.00

Then of the last 200 purchased, 125 were sold and 75 are left.

Next in: April 20	125 @ $8.00	$1,000.00
Cost of Goods Sold		$3,125.00
Ending Inventory	75 @ $8.00	$600.00

Note that the ending inventory had a greater value than when the Averaging method was used and the cost of goods sold was lower. That's because the remaining inventory are the most expensive hammers that were bought.

---

6. Harry's Hardware started the month with 25 wrenches on the shelf with an average per unit value of $3.25. During the month he made these additional purchases:

April 1	100 wrenches @ $3.50
April 10	100 wrenches @ $3.75
April 20	150 wrenches @ $4.00

At the end of the month he had 100 wrenches on the shelf. Calculate the value of the ending inventory and the cost of goods sold using the FIFO method.

Solve It

Using the same purchase information for the hammers shown in the example above, how would you calculate the value of the ending inventory and cost of goods sold using the LIFO inventory method? There was a beginning inventory of 50 hammers purchased at $5 each, ending inventory of 75 hammers. Additional purchases were

Date	Quantity	Per Hammer Price
April 1	150	$5.00
April 10	150	$7.50
April 20	200	$8.00

Since LIFO is last in first out, you would start the calculation with the beginning inventory of 50 hammers at $5 and assume those were sold last. The first hammers sold are the ones that were received last, so you would start with the 200 hammers bought on April 20.

First sold: April 20 purchase	200 @ $8.00	$1,600.00
Next sold: April 10	150 @ $7.50	$1,125.00

Then knowing that you had 75 hammers left, 50 of them would be the oldest units at $5 from the beginning inventory and 25 would be from the purchase on April 1 at $5.

Next sold: April 1	125 @ $5.00	$625.00
Cost of Goods Sold		$3,350.00
Ending Inventory	75 @ $5.00	$375.00

Note that the ending inventory using the LIFO method has the lowest value of the three and the cost of goods sold is the highest.

---

7. Harry's Hardware started the month with 25 wrenches on the shelf with an average per unit value of $3.25. During the month he made these additional purchases:

April 1	100 wrenches @ $3.50
April 10	100 wrenches @ $3.75
April 20	150 wrenches @ $4.00

At the end of the month he had 100 wrenches on the shelf. Calculate the value of the ending inventory and the cost of goods sold using the LIFO method.

Solve It

You can see that as the bookkeeper, it is critical for you to know the inventory valuation method the owner of the company uses. If the cost of goods sold total is higher, then the expenses for the period will be higher and the profit will be lower. That means the owner will pay less taxes because he shows a lower profit. A lower cost of goods sold total will mean the profit will be higher and the taxes will be higher. The Averaging method falls in between these two inventory valuation types.

Buying and monitoring office supplies

In addition to purchasing items for sale, your company also buys office supplies and other items that are needed for the everyday operation of the business. Most likely you will record these purchases by debiting an expense account called Office Supplies and crediting the Cash account (if the purchase was made using cash) or an Accounts Payable account (if the purchase was made on credit).

How carefully you need to monitor the use of the office supplies will depend on your company. Many companies don't require the bookkeeper to monitor anything but the actual expenses and require the management of office supplies to be done by the office manager or supply manager.

Paying Your Bills

After recording the purchases, the bookkeeper takes primary responsibility for making sure that the bills are paid for both the inventory and the supplies purchased. Usually, you will post the bills to Accounts Payable when they arrive, file them in the month or day to be paid, and pay them when they are due.

There are five key functions for paying the bills:

- ✔ Entering the bills into the accounting system
- ✔ Preparing the checks for paying the bills
- ✔ Signing the checks
- ✔ Sending out the payment to the vendors
- ✔ Reconciling the checking account

One person should not be responsible for all these tasks. In fact the person who enters the bills into the accounting system and prepares the checks, should never be the one with the authority to sign the checks. To be even more careful about cash control, it's a good idea to have a third person review the checks against the bills due and actually send the signed checks out to the vendors. By separating these tasks you minimize the risk that business funds will be misused.

A key function of Accounts Payable is to keep track of any discounts your company may be able to take. For example, sometimes a company will offer a 2 percent discount on a bill if paid within 10 days and expect payment in full between 10 days and 30 days. Then, there could be a late penalty of 1.5 percent interest for payments received after 30 days. The Accounts Payable clerk should organize the bills to pay them in time to take advantage of the discount and save his company money.

Q. Suppose a company received a bill for $100,000 on March 31 that was stamped "2% 10 Net 30." What does it mean and when should the bill be paid?

A. The stamp "2% 10 Net 30" means that the company can take a 2 percent discount if paid by April 10; otherwise the full amount is due if paid between April 11 and April 30. To calculate the discount

you would multiply the total amount of the invoice by 2 percent and then subtract that amount from the bill total to find the discounted amount due.

$100,000 \times 2\%$ = $2,000

So the company would save $2,000 if it pays the bill by April 10. Companies can save a lot of money during the month by taking advantage of vendor discounts.

8. Suppose a company received a bill for $500,000 on March 31 that was stamped "3% 10 Net 30." What does it mean and when should the bill be paid?

Solve It

9. Suppose a company received a bill for $100,000 on March 31 that was stamped "2% 15 Net 45." What does it mean and when should the bill be paid?

Solve It

Answers to Problems on Purchasing Goods and Tracking Your Purchases

1 **B:** A periodic inventory system.

2 **A:** A perpetual inventory system.

3 **A:** FIFO. A grocery store would want the first product in (oldest item) to be the first product out (first sold).

4 **D:** Specific Identification. A car dealership usually wants to maintain a specific identification system because each car in the inventory likely has different options and will have a different cost.

5 Here is how you would calculate the ending inventory and cost of goods sold using the averaging method:

Beginning Inventory	25 @ $3.25	$81.25
April 1	100 wrenches @ $3.50	$350.00
April 10	100 wrenches @ $3.75	$375.00
April 20	150 wrenches @ $4.00	$600.00
Total Goods Available for Sale	375 wrenches	$1,406.25
Average Cost per Unit	$1,406.25/375	$3.75
Ending Inventory	100 @ $3.75	$375.00
Cost of Goods Sold	275 @ $3.75	$1,031.25

6 Here is how you would calculate the ending inventory and cost of goods sold using the FIFO method:

Beginning Inventory	25 wrenches @ $3.25	$81.25
Next in: April 1	100 wrenches @ $3.50	$350.00
April 10	100 wrenches @ $3.75	$375.00
April 20	50 wrenches @ $4.00	$200.00
Cost of Goods Sold		$1,006.25
Ending Inventory	100 wrenches @ $4.00	$400.00

7 Here is how you would calculate the ending inventory and cost of goods sold using the LIFO method:

First Sold purchased	April 20: 150 @ $4.00	$600.00
Next Sold purchased	April 10: 100 @ $3.75	$375.00
Next Sold purchased	April 1: 25 @ $3.50	$87.50
Cost of Goods Sold		$1,062.50
Ending Inventory		
	75 from April 1 purchase @ $3.50	$262.50
	25 from Beginning Inventory @ $3.25	$81.25
		$343.75

8 The stamp means that the company can receive a 3 percent discount if it pays the bill in 10 days by April 10 and no discount if the bill is paid between April 11 and April 30. The discount will be $15,000 if paid by April 10. So the bookkeeper should pay the bill by April 10.

9 The stamp means that the company can receive a 2 percent discount if it pays the bill in 15 days by April 15 and no discount if the bill is paid between April 16 and May 15. The discount will be $2,000 if paid by April 15. So the bookkeeper should pay the bill by April 15.

Chapter 8

Calculating and Monitoring Sales

. . . .

. . . .

*Y*ou love to take in money when you run a business. Everyone does. But once that money starts coming in that door it's important that you properly track that cash and credit.

Tracking the cash is not enough, you also must:

✔ Record transactions in your books

✔ Track individual customer accounts

✔ Record any discounts that were offered

✔ Track any returns or allowances that were given to customers

✔ Collect from customers to whom you sell on credit

✔ Monitor customer accounts to be sure they pay on time

✔ Write off accounts from customers who just won't pay

This chapter helps you practice the key elements of tracking your sales, recording them properly in the books, and monitoring all the accounts related to your sales.

Taking in Cash

First you need to know what is cash and what is not. That may sound strange but cash does not only include the dollar bills and coins that you receive. You also count customer checks as cash, as well as items bought on credit cards, as long as those credit cards were not issued by you.

When it comes to buying on credit for the purposes of your bookkeeping, the only purchases that need to be tracked in Accounts Receivable are purchases that involve credit issued by your store. Credit card purchases on credit cards issued by banks or other financial institutions should be listed as cash. In fact, today with the electronic transfer of funds, many companies will see the money show up in their bank account almost immediately after the purchase. It all depends upon how you have set up to receive your money through the bank that handles your credit transactions.

As a bookkeeper, you can get all the information you need to enter cash transactions in the books from your sales receipts. Suppose you are the bookkeeper for a bakery, here is what a sales receipt might look like:

Sales Receipt 2/15/2007

Item	Quantity	Price	Total
Pecan Pie	1	$35.00	$35.00
Cheesecake	1	$35.00	$35.00
Pound Cookies	1	$10.00	$10.00
Subtotal Sales			$80.00
Sales Tax @ 7%			$5.60
Total Sales			$85.60
Cash Paid			$90.00
Change			$4.40

Q. So how would you use this information to develop an entry for your bookkeeping system that would enable you to record this sales transaction in your books?

A. The key numbers you need to use are Total Sales, Subtotal Sales, and Sales Tax. Here is what the bookkeeping entry would look like:

	Debit	Credit
Cash in Checking	$85.60	
Sales		$80.00
Sales Tax Collected		$5.60

Cash receipts for 2/25/2007

The information from this entry would be recorded in your Sales Journal. For more information about Sales Journals and other types of journals you need to maintain, read Chapter 5. Note that you would enter a Debit to the Cash in Checking account and a Credit to the Sales and Sales Tax Collected accounts. An equal amount was posted to both the Debits as there was to the Credits. That should always be true. Your bookkeeping entries should always be in balance. These entries would increase the amount in all three accounts. To understand more about how Debits and Credits work read Chapter 2.

Most likely when you work for a company, you will get a summary of total sales for the day and may not necessarily need to add up each receipt. It all depends on the types of cash registers used in your store. The entry into your books would most likely be a total of cash sales on a daily basis.

1. How would you record this transaction in your books, if you were the bookkeeper for a hardward store?

Sales Receipt 2/25/2007

Item	Quantity	Price	Total
Hammer	1	$15.00	$15.00
Paint Brushes	5	$5.00	$25.00
Paint	2 Gallons	$10.00	$20.00
			$60.00
Sales Tax @ 7%			$4.20
Total Sale			$64.20
Paid by Visa Credit Card			$64.20

Solve It

2. How would you record this transaction in your books, if you were a bookkeeper for an office supply store?

Sales Receipt 3/05/2007

Item	Quantity	Price	Total
Paper	2 boxes	$15.00	$30.00
Print Cartridge	1	$25.00	$25.00
Hanging Files	2 boxes	$10.00	$20.00
			$75.00
Sales Tax @ 6%			$4.50
Total Sale			$79.50
Paid by Personal Check			$79.50

Solve It

3. How would you record this transaction in your books, if you were a bookkeeper for an office supply store?

Sales Summary for 3/05/2007

Item	Quantity	Price	Total
Paper	10 boxes	$15.00	$150.00
Print Cartridges	5	$25.00	$125.00
Hanging Files	7 boxes	$10.00	$70.00
Envelopes	10 boxes	$7.00	$70.00
Pens	20 boxes	$8.00	$160.00
			$575.00
Sales Tax @ 6%			$34.50
Total Cash Sales			$609.50

Solve It

You can also track inventory using the information collected in the sales receipt. I talk more about that in Chapter 7.

Selling on Credit

Many stores also decide to allow their customers to buy using credit offered directly by the store. In these cases the account is not offered by a bank, but instead by the store owner. This gives the store owner the ability to be more flexible about the credit terms and may help to attract customers who otherwise couldn't buy items in the store. For example, a church may have different members who pick up baked goods for church events. The church can authorize certain people to charge to the church account.

If you are the bookkeeper for a company that does allow customers to buy on credit, you will be responsible for recording the sales transactions, as well as maintaining the individual records of customers who buy on store credit.

As a bookkeeper, you also can get all the information you need to enter credit transactions in the books from your sales receipts. The key difference will be the information provided on a receipt for a credit transaction. You will find information about the customer and his account number on the receipt. You can use this additional information to record transactions in the customer's records so you will be able to bill the customer at a later date.

Suppose you are the bookkeeper for a bakery, which does allow customers to buy on credit. Here is what a sales receipt might look like:

Sales Receipt #456 First Baptist Church		2/15/2007 Account #10356	
Item	**Quantity**	**Price**	**Total**
Pecan Pie	1	$35.00	$35.00
Cheesecake	1	$35.00	$35.00
Pound Cookies	1	$10.00	$10.00
			$80.00
Sales Tax @ 7%			$5.60
Total Sale			$85.60

Q. So how would you use this information to make a entry in your bookkeeping system to record this sales transaction?

A. The key numbers you need to use are Total Sales, Subtotal Sales, and Sales Tax. You also need the customer name and account number. Here is what the bookkeeping entry would look like:

	Debit	Credit
Accounts Receivable	$85.60	
Sales		$80.00
Sales Tax Collected		$5.60

Credit receipts for 2/25/2007

In addition to recording the sales transaction in your Sales Journal, you would also need to record the transaction in the customer's account. That account could be maintained on a computer worksheet, in a paper journal, or on cards for each customer. Whichever way your company tracks individual customer accounts, here's the entry that you would need to make to the account of the First Baptist Church:

2/15/2007   Baked Goods — Sales Receipt #456 $85.60

When you record a transaction in a customer's account, you want to be sure you have enough identifying information to be able to find the original sales transaction in case the customer questions the charge when you send the bill at the end of the month. In the section, "Collecting from Your Customers" below, I show you how to use this information to bill and collect from your customers.

4. How would you record this credit transaction in your books, if you were the bookkeeper for a hardward store?

Sales Receipt 2/25/2007, Joe Tester, Account #789

Item	Quantity	Price	Total
Hammer	1	$15.00	$15.00
Paint Brushes	5	$5.00	$25.00
Paint	2 Gallons	$10.00	$20.00
			$60.00
Sales Tax @ 7%			$4.20
Total Sale			$64.20

Solve It

5. How would you record this credit transaction in your books, if you were a bookkeeper for an office supply store?

Sales Receipt 3/05/2007, Sue's Insurance Agency, Account #156			
Item	*Quantity*	*Price*	*Total*
Paper	2 box	$15.00	$30.00
Print Cartridge	1	$25.00	$25.00
Hanging Files	2 boxes	$10.00	$20.00
			$75.00
Sales Tax @ 6%			$4.50
Total Sale			$79.50

Solve It

6. How would you record this transaction in your books, if you were a bookkeeper for an office supply store? What additional information would you need?

Sales Summary for 3/05/2007			
Item	*Quantity*	*Price*	*Total*
Paper	10 boxes	$15.00	$150.00
Print Cartridges	5	$25.00	$125.00
Hanging Files	7 boxes	$10.00	$70.00
Envelopes	10 boxes	$7.00	$70.00
Pens	20 boxes	$8.00	$160.00
			$575.00
Sales Tax @ 6%			$34.50
Total Cash Sales			$159.50
Total Credit Card Sales			$200.00
Total Store Credit Sales			$250.00
Total Sales			$609.50

Solve It

Checking Your Register

You want to be sure that none of your cashiers make mistakes during the day in giving change to customers. You also want to be sure that your cashiers don't decide to pocket any of the cash for themselves.

You monitor cash by knowing exactly how much cash was in the register at the beginning of the day and then checking how much cash is left at the end of the day. You should count the cash at the end of the day as soon as all sales transactions have been completed. You should also print out a summary of all transactions. In many companies the sales manager will actually cash out the register at night working with the cashiers and give you the copy of the completed cash-out form.

After you get that information complete a cash-out form looks something like this:

Cash Register: _____	Date: _____	
Receipts	*Sales*	*Cash in Register*
Beginning Cash	_____	_____
Cash Sales	_____	_____
Credit Card Sales	_____	_____
Store Credit Sales	_____	_____
Total Sales	_____	_____
Minus Sales on Credit	_____	_____
Total Cash Received	_____	_____
Total Cash that Should be in Register		_____
Actual Cash in Register		_____
Difference		_____

Q. Using the sales summary from Question 6 and knowing that you begain the day with $100 in the register and ended the day with $264.50 in the register is the ending cash total correct?

A. Complete the cash-out form below:

Cash Register: Sales Summary Date: 3/5/2007

Receipts	Sales	Cash in Register
Beginning Cash		$100.00
Cash Sales	$159.50	
Credit Card Sales	$200.00	
Store Credit Sales	$250.00	
Total Sales	$609.50	
Minus Sales on Credit	($450.00)	
Total Cash Received		$159.50
Total Cash that Should be in Register		$259.50
Actual Cash in Register		$264.50
Difference		Overage of $5.00

So in this example, with the cash remaining in the cash register, the cashier actually took in $5 more than needed. This was most likely an error in giving change.

7. Use the information in this the Cash Register summary to complete the blank cash-out form below. Also assume that the cash register had $100 at the beginning of the day and $316.10 at the end of the day. Is there a difference between how much should be in the register and how much is there?

Cash Register Summary for Jane Doe on 3/15/2007

Item	Quantity	Price	Total
Paper	20 boxes	$15.00	$300.00
Print Cartridges	10	$25.00	$250.00
Envelopes	10 boxes	$7.00	$70.00
Pens	20 boxes	$8.00	$160.00
			$780.00
Sales Tax @ 6%			$46.80
Total Cash Sales			$226.80
Total Credit Card Sales			$200.00
Total Store Credit Sales			$400.00
Total Sales			$826.80

Cash Register: _____	Date: _____	
Receipts	*Sales*	*Cash in Register*
Beginning Cash	_____	_____
Cash Sales	_____	_____
Credit Card Sales	_____	_____
Store Credit Sales	_____	_____
Total Sales	_____	_____
Minus Sales on Credit	_____	_____
Total Cash Received	_____	_____
Total Cash that Should be in Register		_____
Actual Cash in Register		_____
Difference		_____

Discounting Sales

You may find one other twist to recording sales. Sometimes a store will offer discounts during a sale. You want to keep track of your sales discounts separately, so you know how much money your company lost to discounting over the year. While sales discounts certainly generate traffic, it's important to carefully track how frequently you needed to offer these discounts to encourage traffic or stay competitive with other similar retail stores.

You may find you need to adjust your retail prices to better meet the actual going price on the market, which means you may need to adjust your anticipated profit levels for the year. If your project does come in below what you expect, you will then have the detailed information you need to determine what impacted your sales revenue.

As you record a transaction in your books, you will add an account called Sales Discounts to track any discounts you offer throughout the year.

Q. How would you record this sales transaction?

Sales Receipt 2/15/2007			
Item	*Quantity*	*Price*	*Total*
Pecan Pie	1	$35.00	$35.00
Cheesecake	1	$35.00	$35.00
Pound Cookies	1	$10.00	$10.00
Sales Discount @ 10%			$80.00 (8.00)
			$72.00
Sales Tax @ 7%			$5.04
Total Sales			$77.04
Cash Paid			$80.00
Change			$2.96

A. Here is what the bookkeeping entry would look like:

	Debit	*Credit*
Cash in Checking	$77.04	
Sales Discount	$8.00	
Sales		$80.00
Sales Tax Collected		$5.04

Cash receipts for 2/15/2007

Note that in this situation, the cash in the checking amount is actually less than the sales amount to compensate for the lost revenue for the sales discount. Yet when you total the debit and credit entries they are equal — both total to $85.04.

8. How would you record this transaction in your books, if you were a bookkeeper for an office supply store?

Sales Receipt 3/05/2007			
Item	*Quantity*	*Price*	*Total*
Paper	2 box	$15.00	$30.00
Print Cartridge	1	$25.00	$25.00
Hanging Files	2 boxes	$10.00	$20.00
			$75.00
Sales Discount @ 20%			$15.00
			$60.00
Sales Tax @ 6%			$3.60
Total Cash Sale			$63.60

Solve It

9. How would you record this credit transaction in your books, if you were a bookkeeper for an office supply store?

Sales Summary for 3/05/2007			
Item	*Quantity*	*Price*	*Total*
Paper	10 boxes	$15.00	$150.00
Print Cartridges	5	$25.00	$125.00
Hanging Files	7 boxes	$10.00	$70.00
Envelopes	10 boxes	$7.00	$70.00
Pens	20 boxes	$8.00	$160.00
			$575.00
Sales Discount @20%			$115.00
			$460.00
Sales Tax @ 6%			$27.60
Total Cash Sales			$162.60
Total Credit Card Sales			$150.00
Total Store Credit Sales			$175.00
Total Sales			$487.60

Solve It

Recording Sales Returns and Allowances

Some customers decide they don't want the products they bought and return them to the store. These sales returns must be tracked separately in your books. Another type of transaction that must be tracked separately are sales allowances, which include sales incentive programs such as gift cards.

Sales returns

Although it might be easier to decide on a no-return policy that would surely result in very unhappy customers; instead, a business owner must decide what the rules will be for sales returns and how they will be handled logistically. Here are common rules for sales returns:

- ✔ Returns will only be allowed within 30 days of purchase.
- ✔ You must have a receipt to return an item.
- ✔ If you return an item without a sales receipt, you can receive only store credit.

The person who owns the business for which you are doing the bookkeeping can set up whatever return policies he sees fit. After the policies are determined, the critical issue is how the sales returns will be monitored internally to be sure the return process is not used by cashiers to pocket extra cash. In most stores, a manager's approval is required for a sales return and the manager should carefully check to see how the customer paid for the item. A customer who paid with cash can receive cash back, but a customer who paid by credit card can only get a credit to that card. Only after a manager approves a return can the cashier give that customer either the cash or the credit to their card. If the store's policy is only to give store credit on returns, then a receipt for the store credit would be given to the customer.

Q. If a customer returns an item he bought, how can he get his money back if a store adopts the common rules described above?

a. If he paid cash, he can get cash back provided he shows a receipt for the purchase.

b. If he paid by credit card, he can get a credit to his card provided he shows a receipt for the purchase.

c. If he doesn't show a receipt, he cannot get his money back he can only get store credit.

d. All of the above.

A. The answer is **d.** All are acceptable options for returns.

10. Who should be able to approve a sales return?

a. The cashier

b. The salesperson

c. A manager

d. The bookkeeper

Solve It

11. When can the cashier give a customer cash after a sales return is approved?

a. Cash can be given in all cases.

b. Cash can only be given back if the customer paid by cash.

c. Cash can only be given back if the customer paid by cash and has a receipt.

d. Cash can only be given back if the customer paid by cash or credit card and has a receipt.

Solve It

Sales allowances

Sales allowances are sales incentives programs to get the customer to come back to the store again. The most popular type of sales allowance today is the gift card. With a gift card the customer pays cash up front and gets a gift card that can be used by the customer or any other person that gets the card. Gift cards are actually a liability for the store because the store got the cash, but the customer is still owed an item in exchange for that cash at some time in the future.

Tracking sales returns and allowances

Often sales returns and allowances are tracked using one account called Sales Returns and Allowances that is subtracted from total Sales. When you see an Income Statement you usually see the term "Net Sales." That means that adjustments were made to total sales, which includes this subtraction for sales returns and allowances.

Q. A customer returns a blouse she bought for $40 using cash. She has a receipt showing when she made the original purchase. There is a 6% sales tax. How would you record that transaction in the books?

A. The transaction would be recorded this way:

	Debit	Credit
Sales Returns and Allowances	$40.00	
Sales Taxes Collected	$2.40	
Cash in Checking		$42.40

When you return the amount of the purchase to the customer you must also adjust that amount by adding the taxes the customer paid and subtracting those taxes from Sales Taxes Collected. This transaction would increase the balance in the Sales Returns and Allowances account, would decrease the balance in the Sales Taxes Collected account, and would decrease the amount in the Cash account.

---

12. A customer returns a pair of pants he bought for $35 using a credit card. He has a receipt showing when he made the original purchase. There is a 6% sales tax. How would you record that transaction in the books?

Solve It

13. A customer returns a toy she bought for $25 using cash and has a receipt for the purchase. There is a 6% sales tax. How would you record that transaction in the books?

Solve It

Monitor Collections from Your Customers

Whenever your company sells to customers on credit, you will need to monitor how quickly your customers are paying their bills. You also need to keep track of customers who aren't paying on time. As you do your bills at the end of the month, make a list of all your customers and how much money they have outstanding in their accounts and the date on which the original charge was made.

Here is a list for five customers who bought on credit from the office supply store and have not yet paid their bills as of 3/31/2007:

Customer	Date of Purchase	Amount Purchased
Sue's Insurance Company	3/5/2007	$79.50
Joe Tester	2/25/2007	$64.20
First Baptist Church	2/15/2007	$85.60
	3/15/2007	$67.20
Jane Doe	1/15/2007	$49.50
Harry Man	12/23/2007	$89.20

In addition to sending out invoices on April 2, you should also prepare an Aging Summary for your manager that summarizes all your customers that owe money. You would group this summary based on time of purchase.

Q. Prepare an Aging Summary report as of March 31 for all outstanding customer accounts.

A. Here is what an Aging Summary report would look like:

Aging Summary: As of March 31, 2007				
Customer	Current	31–60 Days	61–90 Days	>90 Days
Sue's	$79.50			
Tester		$64.20		
First Baptist	$67.20	$85.60		
Jane Doe			$49.50	
Harry Man				$89.20
Totals	$146.70	$147.80	$49.50	$89.20

You can quickly see who is behind in their bills and how much old debt you have on your books. You should give a copy of this information to your manager, as well as the sales or store manager so they can make decisions about whether or not they want to continue offering credit to customers who aren't paying their bills. Your company will also need to establish a collections process.

14. Use the information from the account list below to set up an Aging Summary as of 4/30/2007:

Customer	Date of Purchase	Amount Purchased
Sarah Smith	4/5/2007	$37.85
Joe James	3/15/2007	$63.20
Manny's Restaurant	3/20/2007	$135.20
Manny's Restaurant	4/15/2007	$128.75
Harry Harris	2/25/2007	$49.50
Maury Man	1/5/2007	$89.20

Solve It

Writing Off Bad Accounts

Sometimes your company will have to accept the fact that you'll never collect the money from some customers. When that happens you'll need to write off the loss as a bad debt. Each company sets its own policy on how long they will keep an account on the books before it is written off as bad debt.

Q. Suppose your company determines that it will write off bad debt after it's six months past due. After completing your Aging Summary on 4/30/2007, you find that you have two accounts totaling $157.45 that are more than 6 months past due. How would you record that information in your books:

A.

Debit	Credit
Bad Debt	$157.45
Accounts Receivable	$157.45

Accounts written off for bad debt as of 4/30/2007

15. You discover after compiling your Aging Report for 6/30/2007 that you have an account that is more than six months past due for a total of $125.65. Your company policy is that you write off bad debt once an account is more than six months late. How would you record this transaction in your books?

Solve It

Answers to Problems on Calculating and Monitoring Sales

1

	Debit	Credit
Cash in Checking	$64.20	
Sales		$60.00
Sales Tax Collected		$4.20

Cash receipts for 2/25/2007

2

	Debit	Credit
Cash in Checking	$79.50	
Sales		$75.00
Sales Tax Collected		$4.50

Cash receipts for 3/5/2007

3

	Debit	Credit
Cash in Checking	$609.50	
Sales		$575.00
Sales Tax Collected		$34.50

Cash receipts for 3/5/2007

4

	Debit	Credit
Accounts Receivable	$64.20	
Sales		$60.00
Sales Tax Collected		$4.20

Credit receipts for 2/25/2007

5

	Debit	Credit
Accounts Receivable	$79.50	
Sales		$75.00
Sales Tax Collected		$4.50

Credit receipts for 3/5/2007

6

	Debit	Credit
Cash in Checking	$359.50	
Accounts Receivable	$250.00	
Sales		$575.00
Sales Tax Collected		$34.50

Credit receipts for 3/5/2007

Note that you add the total for Cash and Credit Card Sales to find out how much you should add to Cash in Checking. Only the items bought through store credit are recorded in Accounts Receivable.

7 Here is how you would complete the cash out form.

Cash Register: Jane Doe	Date: 3/15/2007	
Receipts	*Sales*	*Cash in Register*
Beginning Cash		$100.00
Cash Sales	$226.80	
Credit Card Sales	$200.00	
Store Credit Sales	$400.00	
Total Sales	$826.80	
Minus Sales on Credit	$600.00	
Total Cash Received		$226.80
Total Cash that Should be in Register		$326.80
Actual Cash in Register		$316.10
Difference		Shortage of $10.70

8

	Debit	Credit
Cash in Checking	$63.60	
Sales Discount	$15.00	
Sales		$75.00
Sales Tax Collected		$3.60

Cash receipts for 3/5/2007

9

	Debit	Credit
Cash in Checking	$487.60	
Sales Discount	$115.00	
Sales		$575.00
Sales Tax Collected		$27.60

Cash receipts for 3/5/2007

10 **C:** Manager. In order to protect store assets, a manager's approval should be required for all sales returns.

11 **C:** A person who wants to return an item and get cash must have paid for the item with cash originally and must show a receipt.

12 The entry would be

	Debit	Credit
Sales Returns and Allowances	$35.00	
Sales Taxes Collected	$2.10	
Cash in Checking		$37.10

Even though the customer is receiving a credit on his credit card, you would show this refund by crediting your "Cash in Checking" account. Remember when a customer uses a credit card the card is processed by the bank and cash is deposited in the store's checking account.

13 The entry would be

	Debit	Credit
Sales Returns and Allowances	$25.00	
Sales Taxes Collected	$1.50	
Cash in Checking		$26.50

14 Here is what an Aging Summary report would look like:

Aging Summary: As of April 30, 2007

Customer	Current	31–60 Days	61–90 Days	>90 Days
Sarah Smith	$37.85			
Joe James		$63.20		
Manny's	$128.75	$135.20		
Harry Harris			$49.50	
Maury Man				$89.20
Totals	$166.60	$198.40	$49.50	$89.20

15

	Debit	Credit
Bad Debt	$125.65	
Accounts Receivable		$125.65

Accounts written off for bad debt as of 6/30/2007

Chapter 9

Paying Your Employees

· ·

· ·

*M*ost businesses do hire employees. Unless the business has only one employee (the owner), it most likely will pay some employees, offer benefits, and manage a payroll. In this chapter you will explore employee staffing issues the bookkeeper may need to manage. In addition you'll practice key aspects of the payroll function that fall to the bookkeeper.

Setting Up Payroll

In many small companies, the bookkeeper takes the responsibility for being certain that all needed government forms are completed when a new person is hired. These forms include

- ✔ **Employer Identification Number:** Every company must have an Employer Identification Number (EIN) to complete all the paperwork that must be filed with the state and federal government. To get this number, a company must submit an SS-4. If your company doesn't have an EIN, you can get a copy of the from at `http://www.irs.gov/pub/irs-pdf/fss4.pdf`.

- ✔ **W-4:** Each employee must complete a W-4, "Employee's Withholding Allowance Certificate." You've probably completed many of these during your working life. It's the form where you tell the employer how much to take out in taxes. As the bookkeeper you need one of these for each employee so you know how to calculate the taxes to be taken out of each paycheck. You can get a copy of this form at `http://www.irs.gov/pub/irs-pdf/fw4.pdf`.

- ✔ **I-9:** This form is required to prove eligibility to work in the U.S. You must be sure each employee has completed this form before they can start to work for your company. Civil penalties can be imposed on employers who fail to comply with this requirement. You can get a copy of this form at `http://www.uscis.gov/files/form/i-9.pdf`.

- ✔ **W-5:** Some employees may be eligible for an Earned Income Credit (EIC), which is a tax credit that refunds some of the money that an employee might otherwise need to pay toward Social Security and Medicare. This reduces the tax bill for low-income workers. Form W-5 is used to declare eligibility for the EIC. As the bookkeeper, after this form is filed you would then reduce the taxes you take from the employee's paycheck. You can get a copy of this form at `http://www.irs.gov/pub/irs-pdf/fw5.pdf`.

Q. What number must every employer have in order to file government and state employee tax forms?

   a. Employer Identification Number (EIN)

   b. Tax Collector Number

   c. Government Identification Number

   d. A number is not needed

A. The answer is **a,** Employer Identification Number (EIN).

---

1. If an employee is eligible for a reduction of Social Security and Medicare taxes, what form must he complete in order for you to reduce the taxes taken out of his check?

   a. W-4

   b. W-5

   c. I-9

   d. EIN

Solve It

2. When an employee starts work and you need to document that the employee is eligible to work in the United States, what form must be completed by the new employee?

   a. W-4

   b. W-5

   c. I-9

   d. EIN

Solve It

---

3. In order for you as the bookkeeper to know how much to take out in employee taxes, what form must every employee complete when they are hired?

   a. W-4

   b. W-5

   c. I-9

   d. EIN

Solve It

Determining pay periods

Companies operate using four different pay periods. As the bookkeeper you will need to keep track of how frequently each employee is paid. Often a company will pay hourly employees (employees paid based on an hourly rate) on a weekly or biweekly basis and salaried employees (employees paid based on a set monthly income rather than based on the number of hours worked) on a semimonthly or monthly basis. Here are the frequencies for payroll based on pay periods:

Weekly: Employees receive a paycheck each week and payroll must be done 52 times a year.

Biweekly: Employees receive a paycheck every two weeks and payroll must be done 26 times a year.

Semimonthly: Employees receive a paycheck twice a month, commonly on the 15th day of the month and the last day of the month. Payroll must be done 24 times per year.

Monthly: Employees receive one paycheck per month and payroll must be done 12 times a year.

In addition to knowing a person's pay period, you also must know whether the person is an exempt or nonexempt employee. Exempt employees are exempt from the Fair Labor Standards Act (FLSA), which sets the rules for minimum wages, equal pay, overtime pay, and child labor laws. Exempt employees often work more than 40 hours a week, but get no overtime pay. Nonexempt employees must be paid time and one-half for any hours worked over 40 hours in a seven-day period. As the bookkeeper, you'll need to review employee work hours for all nonexempt employees and calculate overtime due.

4. If you work for a company that pays its employees every two weeks, what type of payroll would you prepare?

a. Weekly

b. Biweekly

c. Semimonthly

d. Monthly

Solve It

5. If you work for a company that pays its employees on the 15th and 30th of the month, what type of payroll would you prepare?

a. Weekly

b. Biweekly

c. Semimonthly

d. Monthly

Solve It

6. True or false: If employees who work more than 50 hours must be paid overtime, they are considered exempt employees.

Solve It

Collecting Employee Payroll Taxes

Another key responsibility of the bookkeeper when preparing payroll is to collect all the federal and state taxes due from the employees. Yes, employers do play tax collector when they dole out the paychecks and must reduce those checks by the amount of taxes due. In fact, you will collect taxes for Social Security, Medicare, Federal withholding, and, if applicable, state or local withholding.

Each employee must pay Social Security taxes of 6.2 percent on earned income up to the cap of $97,500 in 2007. This amount is adjusted for inflation each year by the Social Security Administration. An employee who earns more than $97,500 does not pay Social Security on earnings over $97,500. The Social Security cap is adjusted each year. As the bookkeeper you will need to keep track of the annual cap so you know when you can stop taking out Social Security taxes for higher income employees.

The calculation of Social Security taxes is simple. You multiply the gross amount (the full amount of pay before any deductions) of the check times 6.2 percent. Here is the calculation for an employee that earned $1,000 in a pay period:

$1,000 × 0.062 = $62.00

Medicare taxes also must be taken out. Each employee pays 1.45 percent of his earned income toward Medicare. There is no cap on Medicare taxes. The calculation is similar to that for Social Security. You multiply the gross amount of the check times 1.45 percent. Here is the calculation for Medicare taxes on a gross check of $1,000:

$1,000 × 0.0145 = $14.50

Your work in calculating federal withholding taxes (income taxes), as well as state or local taxes is much more complex. You not only have to know what the tax rate is for an employee, but you also must know how many withholding allowances the employee claims. You'll find the number of withholding allowances claimed on the W-4 the employee filed at the time he was hired.

You can image how difficult it would be if you had to calculate taxes for each employee taking all these factors into consideration. Luckily the government does make it easier for you and prepares tax tables based on wages and the number of allowances claimed. You can find all the federal rules for employers, as well as the tax tables, in Publication 15, "IRS Employer's Tax Guide" (www.irs.gov/publications/p15/index.html). At the back of the guide in the section called additional materials are tables you can use to find an employee's tax obligation. Table 9-1 is a sample of a portion of that table for an employee that earns $1,000 per week.

Table 9-1		Portion of an IRS Tax Table for Employers										
If the wages are:		*and the Number of Allowances claimed is:*										
At least	**But less than**											
		0	**1**	**2**	**3**	**4**	**5**	**6**	**7**	**8**	**9**	**10**
1,000	1,010	172	156	139	123	107	90	77	67	57	48	38
1,010	1,020	174	158	142	125	109	93	79	69	59	49	39
1,020	1,030	177	161	144	128	112	95	80	70	60	51	41

The federal withholding tax that must be deducted can be found by looking in the column that matches the withholding allowances claimed. For example if Sue earned $1,000 per week and claimed 3 withholding allowances, then the amount of tax you would need to take out of her check would be $139.

In addition to federal withholding taxes, you may have to calculate state and local taxes, if appropriate. You can find contact information for each state's taxing authority online at www.payroll-taxes.com.

Q. Mary earns $1,000 per week and claims 1 withholding deduction. Calculate her Social Security, Medicare, and federal withholding taxes. Then calculate her pay check after taxes have been taken out.

A.

Social Security	1000×0.062	=	$62.00
Medicare	1000×0.0145	=	$14.50
Federal Withholding		=	$156.00
Paycheck minus taxes	$1,000–$62.00–$14.50–$156.00	=	$767.50

7. Carl earns $1,015 per week and claims 4 withholding deductions. Calculate his Social Security, Medicare, and federal withholding taxes. Then calculate his paycheck after taxes have been taken out.

Solve It

8. Karen earns $1,025 per week and claims 2 withholding deductions. Calculate his Social Security, Medicare, and federal withholding taxes. Then calculate his paycheck after taxes have been taken out.

Solve It

9. Tom earns $1,020 per week and claims 7 withholding deductions. Calculate his Social Security, Medicare, and federal withholding taxes. Then calculate his paycheck after taxes have been taken out.

Solve It

Figuring Out Net Pay

Taxes are not the only things you will be deducting from a person's paycheck. Many companies provide health insurance benefits, but expect the employee to pay part of the cost. Each employee will designate the type of insurance they want, and you'll need to keep track of how much to take out of his check each pay period. If your company offers other benefits such as retirement plans, life insurance, dependent care assistance, and education assistance, you'll need to deduct any employee costs of those benefits from the check as well.

Many of these benefits are exempt from taxes, so that will reduce the amount of the gross pay that must be used when calculating employee withholding taxes. For example, suppose Fred earns $1,300 per week and puts $200 per week in his tax-exempt retirement savings, $55 goes toward tax-exempt health insurance coverage, $15 goes toward tax-exempt life insurance coverage and $10 goes toward tax-exempt long-term care coverage. So his taxable amount will then be only $1,020. As the bookkeeper you would use the $1,020 to figure out his withholding taxes.

Calculating Payroll

Calculating paychecks will vary depending upon pay period, whether an employee is hourly or salaried, and whether the employee is exempt or no exempt. You also may have some employees that are paid by commission or by partial salary and commission. These variations in pay can make preparing payroll a nightmare for the bookkeeper.

Calculating pay for hourly employees

When you are calculating paychecks for hourly employees, you need to know whether they are exempt or nonexempt. Most hourly employees are nonexempt and are entitled to overtime pay. You also need to know their hourly rate and the number of hours they worked each week in the pay period.

0. Suppose Jack, who is paid weekly, earns $12 per hour and worked 48 hours last week. How would you calculate his gross paycheck?

A. You would separate the amount of timed work at regular pay, 40 hours, from the time worked at overtime pay 8 hours. Then you would calculate the gross paycheck this way:

> 40 hours regular pay × $12 per hour = $480
>
> 8 hours overtime pay × $ 12 per hour × 1.5 overtime rate = $144
>
> Gross pay check $480 + $144 = $624

10. Suppose John, who gets paid biweekly, earns $15 per hour. He worked 40 hours in the first week of the pay period and 45 hours in the second week of the pay period. How much was his gross pay?

Solve It

11. Suppose Ann, who gets paid biweekly, earns $13 per hour. She worked 42 hours in the first week and 46 hours in the second week of the pay period. How much was her gross pay?

Solve It

Calculating pay for salaried employees

Calculating pay for salaried employees can be much easier than hourly employees, since most are not eligible for overtime pay. If you do have salaried employees that are eligible for overtime pay, then you would need to calculate an hourly pay rate for these employees and use that pay rate to calculate the overtime pay.

12. Suppose John makes $30,000 per year and is paid semimonthly. He is an exempt employee. How much would his gross pay be each pay period?

Solve It

13. Suppose Ann makes $42,000 per year and is paid monthly. She is an exempt employee. How much would her gross pay be each pay period?

Solve It

Calculating paychecks for commissioned employees

Some employees' pay will be based on their sales performance and they will receive a commission based on that performance. The employee could be paid on full commission, which would mean all his pay is based on the volume of sales, or he could have a base salary plus commission.

If the employee has a base salary plus commission, then he would get a set amount per month plus a commission based on his sales volume. Full commission employees usually get a greater percentage of their sales volume in commission than employees who earn a base salary plus commission.

To calculate a paycheck for a commissioned employee you need to know his commission percentage, the volume of his sales, and whether or not he has a base salary.

Q. Suppose Jack is a full commission sales person and he earns 10% commission on his sales volume, what would be the amount of his gross paycheck if he is paid on a monthly basis and his monthly sales volume was $60,000?

A. Jack's pay would be calculated by multiplying the sales volume times his commission percentage:

$60,000 × 10% = $6,000

14. Jane earns a base salary of $2,000 plus 5 percent on her sales volume. She is paid on a monthly basis. What would her gross paycheck be if her sales volume was $60,000?

Solve It

15. Jim earns a base salary of $1,500 plus 3 percent on his sales volume. He is paid monthly. What would his gross paycheck be if his sales volume was $75,000?

Solve It

Calculating paychecks for employees who earn tips

One other complication to calculating payroll involves employees who earn tips. In most places where tips are earned, such as a restaurant, the employee earns less than the minimum wage per hour and the employer must prove that the employee earns at least the minimum wage. The federal minimum wage is $5.15 per hour, but many states have increased that minimum wage requirement, so you will need to check the laws in your state.

Restaurants commonly pay employees between $2.50 and $5 per hour plus tips. They then must prove their employees earn at least enough in tips to match the minimum wage requirements in the state in which they operate. For restaurants this can be relatively easy today because many customers pay their bills with credit cards and the restaurant can use those credit card bills to show the tips earned. When you calculate the employee's taxes, those taxes must be calculated on both the base salary and tips earned.

When you prepare paychecks for employees who earn tips you will only be paying them their hourly wage, since the tips are collected each night, but you will have to deduct taxes based on the combined hourly rate of taxes and tips.

Q. If Ann earns $3.00 per hour plus $5 per hour in tips, what would her gross paycheck be and what would be the total pay used to calculate her taxes?

A. Her paycheck would be calculated based on her hourly pay.

$3 × 40 hours work = $120

Her taxes would be calculated based on her pay plus tips or $8 per hour.

$8 × 40 hours = $320

17. Sally earns $4.00 per hour plus makes $7 per hour in tips. If she works 40 hours, what will her weekly gross paycheck be and what would be the total pay used to calculate her taxes?

Solve It

18. Betty earns $2.50 per hour plus makes $8 per hour in tips. If she works 40 hours, what would her weekly gross paycheck be and what would be the total pay used to calculate her taxes?

Solve It

Depositing Taxes

Employers must pay the taxes they collect on behalf of their employees to a financial institution authorized to collect those payments for the government or to the Federal Reserve Bank in their area. Most major banks are authorized to collect these deposits. Employers must file IRS Form 941 quarterly to show the number of employees and how much money they were paid, as well as report the taxes collected. Employers use a coupon to deposit the taxes due.

Employers use the coupon to make monthly deposits in the financial institution. The deposit must be made within 15 days after the end of the month in which the employee was paid. For example, employee taxes collected during the month of March must be paid by April 15. Large employers who collect a total of $100,000 or more in a day must deposit funds on the next banking day. Tax payments can also be made electronically to the Federal Tax Payment System.

As you can see payroll can be a mind-boggling task. Many small companies avoid the headache of managing payroll and benefits by outsourcing payroll to a company that specializes in handling it. If you are responsible for payroll, you may want to research the cost of contracting these services and make a case to outsource the work.

Answers to Problems on Paying Your Employees

1 **B:** W-5.

2 **C:** I-9.

3 **A:** W-4.

4 **B:** Biweekly.

5 **C:** Semimonthly.

6 **False:** Exempt employees are exempt form the FLSA. You do not need to pay them overtime.

7 The answer is:

Social Security	$1,015 × .062	=	$62.93
Medicare	$1,015 × .0145	=	$14.72
Federal Withholding		=	$109.00
Paycheck after taxes	$1,015–$62.93–$14.72–$109	=	$828.35

8 The answer is:

Social Security	$1,025 × .062	=	$63.55
Medicare	$1,025 × .0145	=	$14.86
Federal Withholding		=	$144.00
Paycheck after taxes	$1,025– $63.55– $14.86–$144	=	$802.59

9 The answer is:

Social Security	$1,020 × .062	=	$63.24
Medicare	$1,020 × .0145	=	$14.79
Federal Withholding		=	$70.00
Paycheck after taxes	$1,020 – $63.24 – $14.79 – $70	=	$871.97

10 The answer is:

Regular hours	80 × $15	=	$1,200.00
Overtime hours	5 × $15 × 1.5	=	$112.50
Gross pay		=	$1,312.50

11 The answer is:

Regular hours	80 × $13	=	$1,040.00
Overtime hours	8 × $13 × 1.5	=	$156.00
Gross pay		=	$1,196.00

12 Bimonthly pay = $30,000/24 = $1,250

13 Monthly pay = $42,000/12 = $3,500

14 $2,000 + $3,000 ($60,000 × .05) = $5,000

15　$1,500 + $,2250 = $3,750

16　$7,500

17　$11 × 40 = $440

18　$10.50 × 40 = $420

Chapter 10

Paying Employer Taxes and Completing Related Government Reports

. . . .

In This Chapter

▶ Paying employer's share of Social Security and Medicare

▶ Calculating unemployment taxes

▶ Insuring for workman's compensation

▶ Keeping employee records

. . . .

*O*nce a company hires employees it will need to complete regular reports for the government regarding taxes it must pay for the employee (Social Security, Medicare, and federal and state withholding taxes), workman's compensation, and unemployment taxes. In this chapter you will review the employer reporting requirements for companies related to federal, state and local government entities, as well as the records the bookkeeper must keep in order to do these reports.

Paying Social Security and Medicare Taxes

Employers must pay half of the Social Security and Medicare taxes for every employee. So in addition to taking out 6.2 percent for Social Security taxes and 1.45 for Medicare taxes from each employee's paycheck, the employer must pay the same percentages. A total of 12.4 percent goes toward an employee's Social Security record and 2.9 percent goes toward an employee's Medicare record. Calculating those taxes is done in the same way as shown in Chapter 9 for calculating the employee's half.

In Chapter 9 I explain how employers need to use Form 941, "Employer's Federal Tax Return," which must be filed quarterly. Table 10-1 shows you the filing due dates for that form.

Table 10-1	Filing Requirements for Employer's Quarterly Federal Tax Return (Form 941)
Months in Quarter	*Report Due Date*
January, February, March	On or before April 30
April, May, June	On or before July 31
July, August, September	On or before October 31
October, November, December	On or before January 31

Here is the information you must be sure you include on Form 941:

Number of employees who received wages

Total of wages, tips, and other compensation paid to employees

Total of tax withheld from wages, tips, and other compensation

Taxable Social Security and Medicare wages

Total paid out in sick pay

Adjustments for tips and group-term life insurance

Amount of income tax withholding

Advance earned income credit payments made to employees

Amount of tax liability per month

The actual taxes reported on this form will be paid monthly by most employers. In Figure 9-2 I show you the coupon used to pay these taxes to an approved financial institution or to the Federal Reserve Bank in your area. If you collect more than $100,000 on any one day then you'll have to deposit those taxes on the next business day. Employers that collect $200,000 in taxes must deposit the money due electronically through the EFTPS (Electronic Federal Tax Payment System). Employers who fail to pay on time or underpay the amount due can be charged interest and penalties, so you want to be sure you pay on time and pay the amount due.

Q. What form must every employer file with the government to report taxes paid or collected on behalf of employees?

a. Form 941, monthly

b. Form 941, quarterly

c. Form 149, monthly

d. Form 149, quarterly

A. The answer is Form 941 on a quarterly basis. Remember though that the taxes must be deposited monthly and large employers must deposit those taxes even more frequently.

1. What information is reported on Form 941?

a. Total of tax withheld from wages, tips and other compensation

b. Taxable Social Security and Medicare wages

c. Total paid out in sick pay

d. All of the above

Solve It

2. At what point must an employer start to pay taxes collected for employees on a daily basis?

a. Once the employer starts to collect taxes for employees

b. Once the employer collects more than $50,000 in a day

c. Once the employer collects more than $100,000 in a day

d. Once the employer collects more than $200,000 in a day

Solve It

3. Where must the employer deposit taxes collected for employees?

    a. At a Federal Reserve Bank

    b. At an approved financial institution

    c. Pay electronically using EFTPS

    d. Any of three methods provided the amount due is less than $200,000

Solve It

4. What are the dates for paying the taxes withheld from employees?

    a. By Jan. 1, April 1, July 1, and October 1

    b. April 30, July 31, October 31, and January 31

    c. Feb. 1, May 1, August 1, and November 1

    d. Feb. 28, May 31, August 31, and November 30

Solve It

Filing Unemployment Reports and Paying Taxes

Another major tax you must start to pay once your company employs people is unemployment taxes. These taxes are paid into the Federal Unemployment Tax Fund (FUTA) and used to pay unemployment benefits to people who are fired or laid off. Employers contribute to this fund as well as to an unemployment fund in their states.

The FUTA rate for employers is 6.2 percent on the first $7,000 that each employee earns. Luckily you don't have to add the state rate on top of that because the federal government allows you to subtract up to 5.4 percent of the first $7,000 per employee that you pay to the state or a maximum credit of $378 per employee (7,000 x 5.4 percent). The state taxes serve as a credit to the federal taxes due. Each state sets its own unemployment rates. Many states also charge additional fees for administrative costs and job-training programs. You can find the rules for your state at payroll-taxes.com, but to give you an idea of how taxes vary state to state, review Table 10-2.

Table 10-2	Sampling of Unemployment Tax Rates		
State	*Percentage Range*	*For a Salary Up to*	*New Employer Percentage*
California	1.5 to 6.2	$7,000	3.4
Florida	0.12 to 6.4	$7,000	2.7
Nevada	0.25 to 5.4	$24,600	2.95
New York	0.9 to 8.9	$8,500	3.4
Rhode Island	1.4 to 5.4	$14,000	2.9

You can see in Table 10-2 there is a range in the percentage of unemployment taxes the employer must pay per employee. This range is based on the company's employment history and how often the company lays off or fires employees who must then draw unemployment benefits. States calculate your company's FUTA tax rate in four different ways:

✔ **Benefit ratio formula:** Looks at the ratio of benefits collected by former employees to your company's total payrolls over the past three years. Your company's rate depends upon its balance in the state unemployment insurance fund.

✔ **Benefit wage formula:** Looks at the proportion of your company's payroll that's paid to workers who become unemployed and collect benefits and then divides that number by your company's total taxable wages.

✔ **Payroll decline ratio formula:** Looks at the decline in your company's payrolls from year to year or from quarter to quarter.

✔ **Reserve ratio formula:** Looks at your company's balance in the unemployment reserve account, which gives a cumulative representation of its use by your employees that were laid off and paid unemployment.

Each state sets a rate in the middle of the range for new employers, which gets adjusted once they have a hiring history in the state based on the formula that state uses. You can find out which formula your state uses on payroll-taxes.com. To clarify what your company might expect and how to minimize unemployment taxes, sit down with a representative from your state unemployment office and review your state's policies.

Q. Using Table 10-2, calculate the FUTA taxes for a new employer in the state of Florida. He has ten employees. Each earns more than $20,000.

A. The state unemployment rate for new employers is 2.7% up to an income of $7,000, so to calculate the state taxes you would multiply $7,000 × .027 × 10 = $1,890.

The federal unemployment rate is 6.2% up to $7,000 in income, so the Federal unemployment taxes would be calculated by multiplying $7,000 × .062 × 10 = $4,340.

The company can subtract what it pays the state from the amount due the federal government, so it would pay the state $1,890 and pay the federal government $2,450 ($4,340–$1,890).

---

5. Using Table 10-2, calculate the FUTA taxes for a new employer in the state of California. He has ten employees each earns more than $20,000.

Solve It

6. Using Table 10-2, calculate the FUTA taxes for a new employer in the state of Nevada. He has ten employees. Eight earn $20,000 each. One earns $24,000 and one earns $30,000.

Solve It

7. Using Table 10-2, calculate the FUTA taxes for a new employer in the state of New York. He has ten employees. All earn more than $30,000.

Solve It

8. Using Table 10-2, calculate the FUTA taxes for a new employer in the state of Rhode Island. He has ten employees. Eight earn $14,000. One earns $24,000 and one earns $30,000.

Solve It

Employers must file an annual report called "Employer's Annual Federal Unemployment Tax Return" on Form 940 or 940 EZ. The taxes are usually paid quarterly though. In addition to the federal form you will find that your state has a quarterly or annual unemployment form to file. Some states combine the form filed for unemployment and state income taxes. Eight states have no income taxes — Alaska, Nevada, New Hampshire, South Dakota, Tennessee, Texas, Washington, and Wyoming.

Covering Workman's Compensation

Taxes aren't the only thing you have to worry about once you hire employees. You also must figure out what level of workman's compensation insurance you must carry in your state. Every state except Texas requires you to carry the insurance.

Workman's compensation insurance covers employee's who are injured on the job. This coverage pays for the cost of lost income, medical expenses, vocational rehabilitation and, if applicable, death benefits. In Texas, since it does not require the insurance, it allows employees to sue their employers in civil court to recoup the costs of injuries.

Each state sets its own rules specifying how much medical coverage you must provide and how much you must continue to pay an injured worker in salaries or benefits. The state also decides who gets to pick the physicians who can care for injured employees — the employer, the employee, the state agency, or some combination of the three. In most states the insurance is purchased through private insurance companies. For more details about workman's compensation and insurance options go to www.ncci.com, which is the National Council on Compensation Insurance.

Employer's rates vary by the types of business and types of employees working for that business. Your company's rates are calculated based on risks identified in two areas:

- ✔ **Classification of the business:** These classifications are based on the historic rates of risk in different industries. For example, if you operate a business in an industry that has a high rate of employee injury, such as a construction business, your base rate for workman's compensation is higher than that of a company in an industry without a history of frequent employee injury, such as an office that sells insurance.

- ✔ **Classification of the employee:** The National Council on Compensation Insurance (NCCI) publishes classifications of over 700 jobs in a book called the *Scopes Manual*. Most states use this manual to develop the basis for their classifications. For example desk jobs are cheaper to insure than jobs involving the operation of heavy machinery because there are more injuries when operating heavy machinery than working at a desk.

Many small businesses pay more than needed for workman's compensation insurance because they misclassify their employees. Be sure you understand the classification system and properly classify your employee positions before applying for workman's compensation insurance. You can read more about classification at www.ncci.com.

9. In what states must employers carry workman's compensation coverage?

a. New York and New Jersey only

b. California only

c. All states except Texas

d. Not mandated in any state

Solve It

10. Who determines which doctor an injured employee must see?

a. The state, but the doctor can be chosen by the state, the employer, the employee, or a combination of the three, depending on state rules.

b. The employee

c. The employer

d. The state

Solve It

11. When determining your company's rates, what key factors are used?

a. Classification of your business

b. Classification of your employees

c. Both a and b

d. No classifications are involved.

Solve It

Maintaining Employee Records

With all these governmental filings, I'm sure you've realized by now that you must keep very careful personnel records for each of your employees. The detailed information you must have on file for each employee includes

Name, address, phone number, and Social Security number

Department or division within the company

Start date with the company

Pay rate

Pay period

Whether hourly or salaried

Whether exempt or nonexempt

W-4 withholding allowances

Benefits information

Payroll deductions

All payroll activity

You also have to track if the employee wants to change his withholding allowances or asks for benefit changes. It's a good idea to set up an employee journal and keep a page for each employee. The page set up might look like this:

Name: **SS#:**

Address:

Tax Info: (such as, married, 2 withholding allowances)

Pay Info: (such as $10 per hour, nonexempt, biweekly)

Benefits: (such as health insurance, withholding $100 month)

You would then keep a regular summary of the employee's pay history on the page. The page would need at least seven columns, including date of check, taxable wages, Social Security tax, Medicare tax, benefits withholding, federal withholding, state withholding and net check amount. You could add additional columns if you need to track non-taxable wages, benefits, sick time, or vacation time. Table 10-3 shows you what this section of the employee journal page would look like.

Table 10-3	Sample employee wage summary sheet					
Date	**Taxable Wages**	**SS**	**Medicare**	**Fed WH**	**State WH**	**Check**
4/8/2007	$640.00	$39.68	$9.28	$8.62		$582.42
4/22/2007	$640.00	$39.68	$9.28	$8.62		$582.42

If your company does do its payroll using a computer accounting software program, you can maintain these records on computer, but be certain that you back up that system and prepare paper reports of the data periodically for your files.

Answers to Problems on Paying Employer Taxes and Completing Related Government Reports

1 **D:** All of the above.

2 **C:** Once the employer collects more than $100,000 in a day.

3 **D:** Any of three methods provided the amount due is less than $200,000.

4 **B:** April 30, July 31, October 31, and January 31

5 You first calculate state unemployment taxes by multiplying 3.4% times $7,000 \times 10 = \$2,380$

FUTA taxes are $(6.2\% \times \$7,000 \times 10)$ – amount due state ($2,380) = \$1,960$

6 You first calculate state unemployment taxes for the eight employees earning $20,000 by multiplying $\$20,000 \times 2.95\% \times 8 = \$4,720$ (or $590 per employee).

$\$24,000 \times 2.95\% \times 1 = \$708$

$24,600 (for employee earning $30,000) $\times 2.95\% \times 1 = \$725.50$

Since the maximum FUTA credit is $378 per employee and the employer pays more than that per employee, you can subtract $\$378 \times 10$ employees or $3,780 from the amount due the federal government on FUTA $(6.2\% \times \$7,000 \times 10) - \$3,780 = \$560$.

Amount due Nevada: $4,720 + 708 + 725.50 = $6,153.50

7 You first calculate the state unemployment taxes by multiplying $\$8,500 \times 3.4\% \times 10 = \$2,890$

FUTA taxes are $(6.2\% \times \$7,000 \times 10) - \$2,890 = \$1,450$

8 You first calculate state unemployment taxes for the eight employees earning $14,000 by multiplying $\$14,000 \times 2.9\% \times 10 = \$4,060$ (or $406 per employee).

Since the maximum credit for FUTA allowed is $3,780 the amount due FUTA would be $(6.2\% \times \$7,000 \times 10) - \$3,780 = \$560$.

9 **C:** All states except Texas.

10 **A:** The state, but the doctor can be chosen by the state, the employer, the employee or a combination of the three depending on state rules.

11 **C:** Both the classification of your business and your employees are factored in when computing the cost of a business's workman's compensation insurance.

Part IV
Getting Ready for Year's (Or Month's) End

The 5th Wave   By Rich Tennant

"Cooked books? Let me just say you could serve this profit and loss statement with a fruity Zinfandel and not be out of place."

In this part . . .

*E*ventually every accounting period has an end. When that end comes, whether it's the end of a month, a quarter or a year, you'll need to check your work and get ready to close out the period.

I introduce you to the process of preparing your books for closing out the accounting period. You also learn about the key adjustments needed to record depreciation of your assets (a process which tracks the use of your tangible assets, such as cars and buildings), which must be done before you close the books. Plus, you learn how to calculate and record your interest payments and income in your books.

Then I show you how to prove out your books by checking your cash, testing your book's balance and making any needed adjustments or corrections.

Chapter 11

Depreciating Your Assets

· ·

In This Chapter

▶ Exploring depreciation

▶ Pricing assets

▶ Arranging schedules

· ·

As a business uses its assets, the assets eventually get used up. Businesses track the use of their assets by calculating depreciation expnses.

This chapter will introduce you to depreciation and the various methods that are used to calculate it. You'll practice the various depreciation methods and learn how to track them within your bookkeeping system.

Understanding Depreciation

You probably think of depreciation as something that happens to a now car when you drive it off the lot after purchasing it. All of a sudden it's worth 20 to 30 percent less and it's called depreciation. Well, for bookkeeping purposes it's not quite the same thing. Accountants use depreciation to adjust the books based on the aging of a piece of equipment or other asset.

As an asset is used, its useful life is reduced. For example, when you drive a car 15,000 to 20,000 miles a year, you know that eventually it will need more and more repair until finally you decide it's used up and you want to replace it with something new. That happens to manufacturing equipment, furniture, as well as any other business asset held for more than a year. A company needs to track this use of assets to know the value of what it has and also to estimate repair and replacement costs based on the age of its assets.

Not everything can be depreciated. Any item that you expect to use up in a year is not eligible for depreciation. These types of items are written off as expenses instead. You also don't depreciate land. Land does not get used up. While you can't depreciate a building or car you rent or lease, if you do major renovations to a leased property you can depreciate the value of those improvements.

Assets you own that are used for both your business and your personal life can be partially depreciated based on percentage of use. The two most common types of partially depreciated assets for people who own a home business are their car and a portion of their house. For these situations the business owners are primarily looking to take advantage of the tax savings that can be generated by depreciation.

This chapter focuses on depreciation expenses. Depreciation for tax purposes is an entirely different topic. Check with your accountant to find out more information about depreciation methods used for tax purposes or read IRS publication 946, "How to Depreciate Property" (www.irs.gov/publications/p946/index.html).

Q. Businesses depreciate assets to:

a. Take advantage of tax savings

b. Track the use of their assets

c. Project repair and replacement needs

d. All of the above

A. The answer is d. All of the above are correct. Depreciation is a tax deduction. It does calculate the using up of an asset and by knowing the age of its assets, a business can determine expected repair and replacement costs. For example, older assets likely will need more repair and their replacement will be needed much sooner than newer assets.

1. Not all assets can be depreciated. Which of the following assets can be depreciated?

a. Land that you own

b. Renovations to a building you lease

c. Raw materials you buy for manufacturing

d. Car that you use personally

Solve It

2. Which of the following assets cannot be depreciated?

a. Car used for business purposes

b. Machines used for manufacturing

c. Furniture used in your retail store

d. Inventory bought for sale

Solve It

Figuring out the useful life

The first thing you must determine when you need to calculate the depreciation for an asset is how long that asset will be useful to the company. While you can set up your own table for periods of useful life for types of assets in your business, you will have to justify the lifespan you've chosen if it differs from IRS rules. So most businesses use the depreciation recovery periods set up by the IRS, which set an average useful life for business assets as shown in Table 11-1. Some types of business will use a different depreciation schedule. For example, a rental car business may shorten the useful life of a car from five years (as estimated by the IRS in Table 11-1) to two years because its cars are used much more frequently and get used up much quicker than they would in another type of business.

Table 11-1	Depreciation Recovery Periods for Business Equipment
Property Class Recovery Period	*Business Equipment*
3-year property	Tractor units and horses over two years old
5-year property	Cars, taxis, buses, trucks, computers, office machines (faxes, copiers, calculators, and so on), research equipment and cattle
7-year property	Office furniture and fixtures
10-year property	Water transportation equipment, single-purpose agricultural or horticultural structures, and fruit- or nut-bearing vines and trees
15-year property	Land improvements, such as shrubbery, fences, roads, and bridges

Property Class Recovery Period	Business Equipment
20-year property	Farm buildings that are not agricultural or horticultural structures
27.5-year property	Residential rental property
39-year property	Nonresidential real estate, including a home office but not including the value of the land

3. If you buy office furniture, how long is the useful life of that furniture based on the IRS recovery period?

a. 3 years

b. 5 years

c. 7 years

d. 10 years

Solve It

4. If you buy an office building for your business, how long is the useful life of that building based on the IRS recovery period?

a. 15 years

b. 20 years

c. 27.5 years

d. 39 years

Solve It

5. If you buy land for a future office building, how long is the useful life of that land based on the IRS recovery period?

a. 15 years

b. 20 years

c. 39 years

d. Land value is not included when determining the useful life of an asset for depreciation.

Solve It

Determining the cost basis

The other key factor in calculating depreciation is the cost basis of an asset. The equation for cost basis is

> Cost of the fixed asset + Sales tax + Shipping and delivery costs + Installation charges + Other costs (such as commissions or finder's fees) = Cost basis

> Cost of the fixed asset is what you paid for that equipment, furniture, building, vehicle, or any other asset you intend to use for more than 12 months

> Sales tax is the actual taxes you were charged when purchasing that asset

Shipping and delivery includes any charges that you paid to get that asset to your place of business.

Installation charges include any charges you paid to get that asset working in your business. That could include new electrical outlets, carpentry work, or any type of work that was needed to install the new asset.

Other costs include any other costs involved in the purchase of the asset. This can include commissions or finder fees, as well as additional hardware such as wiring or monitors to put a new piece of equipment into operation.

0. Calculate the cost basis of a new desk for your office. You bought the desk for $1,500 and paid $90 in taxes. You paid $50 to have it delivered.

A. Cost basis = $1,500 + $90 + $50 = $1,640

6. Calculate the cost basis for your new car. You bought the car for $25,000 and paid $1,500 in taxes. You also bought car mats for $125 and a tank of gas for $45.

Solve It

7. Calculate the cost basis for your new office building. You paid $300,000 for the building and $200,000 for the commercial land. You paid a Realtor's commission of $20,000 and closing costs of $35,000.

Solve It

8. Calculate the cost basis for the renovations of the office space you just leased. You paid $20,000 for new carpet, you paid $30,000 for new office furniture, you paid $5,000 for painting the space, and you paid a contractor $15,000 to install dry wall to build out the offices.

Solve It

Depreciating Your Assets

Once you know your assets anticipated life span and its cost basis, you can then calculate how much you should write off for depreciation. Depreciation is not a cash expense. The cash expense happens when you buy the asset or a cash inflow can happen when you sell the asset. Depreciation just shows the use of that asset, so it does not involve the use of cash. I show you how to record depreciation in the books below in the section, "Recording Depreciation Expenses."

You actually can choose from four different methods to calculate depreciation — Straight-Line, Sum-of-Years-Digits, Double Declining Balance, and Units of Production. I show you how to calculate each below and then give you a chance to practice.

Straight-line

Straight-line depreciation spreads out the cost of the asset over the entire useful life of an asset. It's the simplest type of depreciation to calculate. The formula is

(Cost of the asset – Salvage) / Estimated useful life = Annual depreciation expense

The salvage value is the value you expect the asset will have when you sell it after you have finished using it for your business. For example, if you buy a car for $25,000 and expect to be able to sell it for $5,000, the salvage value of that car would be $5,000.

Q. Calculate the annual depreciation expense for a car with a cost basis of $25,000 and a $5,000 salvage value using the IRS recovery period.

A. Looking at the IRS chart you see that a car has a 5-year lifespan according to the IRS. So you would calculate straight-line depreciation in this way:

($35,000 – $5,000) = $30,000

$30,000/5 = $6,000 annual depreciation expense

9. Calculate the annual depreciation expense for a copier with a cost basis of $5,000 and a salvage value of $500 using the IRS recovery period.

Solve It

Sum-of-years-digits

Sometimes a business determines that an asset is used up more quickly in the early years, so it decides to use the sum-of-years-digits (SYD) method. This is common for a trucking company when it buys a new truck. The SYD calculation is a three step process:

1. **Find the SYD for the current fiscal year using this formula:**

   N(N + 1) / 2 = SYD (N would be the number of years of useful life). The SYD would be the same each year of calculation.

2. **Find the application fraction using this formula:**

   N/SYD (N would be the number of years remaining of useful life).

3. **Calculate the depreciation expense formula:**

   (Cost – Salvage value) × Applicable fraction = Depreciation expense.

0. Calculate the first year of the depreciation expense for a car that had a cost basis of $35,000 and a salvage value of $5,000 using the sum-of-years-digits depreciation method. Assume the IRS recovery period of 5 years.

A. The answer is:

SYD = 5 (5 + 1) / 2 = 30/2 = 15

Applicable fraction = 5/15 = 1/3

Depreciation expense = ($35,000 – 5,000) × 1/3 = $30,000 × 1/3 = $10,000

10. Calculate the yearly depreciation expense for years 2 to 5 using SYD for a car with a cost basis of $35,000 and a salvage value of $5,000. Assume the IRS recovery period of 5 years.

Solve It

Double-declining balance

Sometimes businesses want to write off an asset even more quickly than they can use the SYD depreciation calculation because they believe the assets lose usefulness faster. In this case they use a method called double-declining balance, which is double the amount of depreciation allowed using straight-line depreciation. You must calculate a depreciation factor the first year you use double-declining depreciation by using this formula:

$2 \times (1\ /\ \text{Estimated useful life}) = \text{Depreciation factor}$. You then multiply that factor by the book value at the beginning of each year. The depreciation factor will be the same for each year of the calculation.

Salvage value should not be subtracted from the book value, but once the book value is equal to the salvage value, you can't depreciate any more.

Q. Calculate the first year of a car's depreciation expense using the double-declining balance method. The cost basis of the car is $35,000 with a salvage value of $5,000. Assume the IRS recovery period of 5 years.

A. The calculation would be

$2 \times (\tfrac{1}{5}) = .40$

Multiply $35,000 \times .40 = $14,000

11. Calculate the depreciation expense using the double-declining balance method for years 2 to 5 for the $35,000 car using the information from the example above. Remember to use book value at the beginning of each year. Since the depreciation was $14,000 in the first year, the book value at the beginning of the second year would be $21,000 and salvage after 5 years is $5,000.

Solve It

Units of production (UOP)

The units of production (UOP) method of deprecation is used primarily in a manufacturing environment and you would not likely need to calculate depreciation expenses manually in that type of environment. Most likely there would be a computer program for calculating depreciation, so I won't set up a problem to practice this calculation.

In this case the number of units to be produced by the machinery is the key factor that a company wants to track rather than the useful life in years. Rather than calculating a depreciation factor you calculate a UOP rate and then the depreciation expense using this two step process:

Find the UOP rate:

(Cost – Salvage value) / Estimated number of units to be produced during the estimated useful life = UOP rate

Find the depreciation expense using this formula:

Units produced during the year × UOP rate = Depreciation expense

Companies who choose to use this method usually have a wide variation in production levels each year.

Setting Schedules

Remembering how much to depreciate for each asset you have in your business can be an overwhelming task. The best way to keep track of what you need to expense each year is to set up a depreciation schedule for each type of asset that lists the date it was put into service, the description of the asset, the cost basis, the recovery period, and the annual depreciation. Table 11-2 is a sample of this type of schedule.

Table 11-2	Depreciation Schedule: Vehicles			
Date Put in Service	**Description**	**Cost**	**Recovery Period**	**Annual Depreciation**
1/5/2006	Black Car	$30,000	5 years	$5,000
1/1/2007	Blue Truck	$25,000	5 years	$4,000

Recording Depreciation Expenses

Recording depreciation expenses can be a simple entry into your accounting system. Most businesses do the entry at the end of a quarter or the end of the year when they close the books. After calculating depreciation expense, here is the type of entry you would use for a depreciation expense of $4,000 for a vehicle:

	Debit	Credit
Depreciation Expense	$4,000	
Accumulated Depreciation		$4,000

Depreciation expense is a line item on the Income Statement (Chapter 16) and Accumulated Depreciation is a line item on the Balance Sheet (Chapter 17).

Answers to Problems on Depreciating Your Assets

1 **B:** Renovations to a building you lease. Land is never depreciated. Raw materials used for manufacturing would be a Cost of Goods Sold and you can't depreciate assets you use personally.

2 **D:** Inventory bought for sale

3 **C:** 7 years

4 **D:** 39 years

5 **D:** Land value is not included when determining the useful life of an asset for depreciation

6 The cost basis for the car would be $25,000 + $1,500 + $125 = $26,625

You cannot include the cost of a tank of gas in the cost basis for the car. Gas would be an operating expense and written off as an expense in the year incurred.

7 The cost basis for the building would be $300,000 + $20,000 + $35,000 = $355,000

You don't include the value of land when calculating the cost basis.

8 The cost basis for office renovations would be $20,000 + $5,000 + $15,000 = $40,000.

New office furniture should be set up in a separate depreciation schedule with a cost basis of $30,000.

9 First subtract the salvage value: $5,000 − $500 = $4,500

Then: $4,500/5 years = $900 annual depreciation

10 You would use SYD = 15

Year 2: Applicable fraction = $\frac{4}{15}$
$30,000 × $\frac{4}{15}$ = $8,000 depreciation expense

Year 3: Applicable fraction = $\frac{3}{15}$
$30,000 × $\frac{3}{15}$ = $6,000 depreciation expense

Year 4: Applicable fraction = $\frac{2}{15}$
$30,000 × $\frac{2}{15}$ = $4,000 depreciation expense

Year 5: Applicable fraction = $\frac{1}{15}$
$30,000 × $\frac{1}{15}$ = $2,000 depreciation expense

11 Your depreciation factor would be .40.

Year 2: $21,000 × .40 = $8,400 depreciation expense

Year 3: $21,000 − $8,400 = $12,600 — book value at the beginning of the year

$12,600 × .40 = $5,040 depreciation expense

Year 4: $12,600 – $5,040 = $7,560

$7,560 × .40 = $3,024, but since the salvage value is $5,000, depreciation expense can only be $2,560. The car would be fully depreciated in Year 4.

Year 5: $0 depreciation expense

Chapter 12

Paying and Collecting Interest

. . . .

In This Chapter

▶ Exploring types of interest

▶ Delving into credit interest

▶ Booking interest

▶ Paying long-term debt interest

▶ Recording interest income

. . . .

*M*ost businesses carry some debt and most pay interest on that debt. Some businesses loan money or other assets and receive interest payments.

This chapter will review the debt types and how to calculate and record interest expenses for each type. You also will be able to practice how to calculate interest calculations and how to track and enter interest payments into the bookkeeping system.

Determining Interest Types

Financial institutions use two different types of interest calculations when determining how much to pay you in interest for money on deposit or calculating how much you will pay them on a loan or credit card — simple interest and compound interest.

Simple interest

Simple interest is easy to calculate. Here's the formula for calculating simple interest:

$$\text{Principal} \times \text{Interest rate} \times n = \text{Interest}$$

Q. Calculate the simple interest earned over three years for a $10,000 savings account earning 3 percent interest per year.

A. $10,000 \times .03 \times 3 = 900

1. What is the simple interest earned over five years for a $20,000 savings account at 3%?

Solve It

2. What is the simple interest earned over seven years on a $5,000 savings account at 5%?

Solve It

Compound interest

Compound interest is more complicated to calculate because interest is not only charged on the amount you have on deposit, it is also calculated on the interest earned during the time you have it on deposit. So when you calculate compound interest you must add the interest earned the previous period to the balance before calculating the interest earned during the new period. Here's the formula for calculating compound interest for a three-year deposit:

Principal × Interest rate = Interest for year one

(Principal + Interest earned) × Interest rate = Interest for year two

(Principal + Interest earned) × Interest rate = Interest for year three

You would repeat this method of calculation for the life of the deposit.

Q. Calculate the compound interest on a $10,000 deposit at 3% for three years.

A. Year one: $10,000 × .03 = $300

Year two: $10,300 × .03 = $309

Year three: $10,609 × .03 = $318.27

Total interest earned in three years = $927.27

3. What is the compound interest earned over five years for a $20,000 savings account compounded annually at 3%?

Solve It

4. What is the compound interest earned over six years on a $5,000 certificate of deposit, compounded annually at 6%?

Solve It

When you are taking a loan, you always want to be sure you will be paying simple interest. When you are opening a savings account or any other type of savings instrument with a financial institution you always want to be sure you will earn compound interest. Even compound interest can be paid differently. Some banks will compound your earnings monthly, which means interest earned will be added to your balance before the next monthly interest calculation. For other types of accounts interest is only compounded annually. So always look for a bank that compounds your savings monthly.

Determining Interest on Debt

Businesses borrow money for both short-term (less than 12 months) and long-term business needs. Short-term debt usually includes credit cards and lines of credit. Long-term debt can include a multi-year loan for a vehicle or 15 or more year loan for a mortgage. Any money paid toward interest in the current year is shown as an interest expense on the Income Statement (see Chapter 16). In this chapter I review how to calculate that interest expense.

Credit cards

As you know from your personal credit cards, if you pay the bill in full at the end of each month, you don't have any interest charges. But, if you don't pay the balance in full each month, interest is charged based on a daily periodic interest rate, which means you start paying interest from the day you make a purchase. The daily periodic rate is calculated by dividing the annual rate by 365 days. Table 12-1 shows you a typical credit card interest charge. You will find a similar table on your credit card bills, but the actual interest rates may be different depending on your credit card agreement.

Table 12-1	Credit Card Interest Chart		
	Avg. Daily Balance	Daily Periodic Rate	Corresponding Annual Rate
Purchases	$XXX	0.034076%	12.44%
Cash	$XXX	0.0452%	16.49%

Q. Using Table 12-1, calculate the interest for a purchase of $150 made on April 15. The month closes on April 30. Assume the bill is not paid in full each month.

A. $150 × 0.034076 = $5.114

5. Using Table 12-1, if you only paid the interest each month and continued to maintain the $150 balance on the credit card, how much interest would you pay during a 12 month period? How much interest would you pay on $150 at 12.44% annually?

Solve It

6. Using Table 12-1, calculate the interest for a cash advance of $150 made on April 15. The month closes on April 30. Assume the bill is not paid in full each month but you do pay the interest.

Solve It

7. Using Table 12-1, if you only paid the interest each month on the cash advance and continued to maintain the $150 balance on the credit card, how much interest would you pay during a 12 month period? How much interest would you pay on $150 at 16.49% annually?

Solve It

After completing problems 1, 2, and 3 you can see that interest compounded daily can be a lot more expensive than a simple annual interest rate. Credit cards are definitely the most expensive way to carry a loan. You won't be calculating interest. Instead you'll be using the amount of interest charged shown on the monthly credit card bill as your interest expense.

Most businesses seek better rates for short-term borrowing by using lines of credit. When using this type of credit line, you draw cash when needed and pay interest on the amount of the loan balance, but it is not compounded daily like a credit card.

Q. A businessman draws $1,000 from his line of credit with an 8% interest rate. How much interest will he pay each month that he has the loan? Assume he pays the total interest due each month, which means the balance will stay constant each month.

A. $1,000 × .08 = $80 – annual interest due

80/12 = $6.67 monthly interest due

8. A businessman draws $5,000 from his line of credit with a 10% interest rate. How much interest will he pay each month that he has the loan? Assume he pays the total interest due each month plus $500. Calculate six months of payments.

Solve It

9. A businessman draws $10,000 from his line of credit with an 8% interest rate. How much interest will he pay each month that he has the loan? Assume he pays the total interest due each month plus $1,000. Calculate six months of payments.

Solve It

Recording Interest on Short-term Debt

Recording interest on short-term debt is simple. When the cash is initially taken out of the account, you would record the cash receipt and the increase in a liability this way:

	Debit	Credit
Cash	$1,500	
Credit Line Payable		$1,500

As you make interest payments, you would record the decrease in Cash and an Interest Expense. If you also paid toward the balance of the loan you would add that to the entry this way:

	Debit	Credit
Credit Line Payable	$150	
Interest Expense	$10	
Cash		$160

Q. How would you record a cash payment on a line of credit of $500 plus $35 interest?

A.

	Debit	Credit
Credit Line Payable	$500	
Interest Expense	$35	
Cash		$535

10. How would you record the cash payment of a credit card if you pay $36 in interest and $200 toward purchases made?

Solve It

11. How would you record the cash payment of a credit card for $47 interest only?

Solve It

12. How would you record the cash payment of $150 of interest only toward a line of credit?

Solve It

13. How would you record the cash payment of $500 plus $85 interest toward a line of credit?

Solve It

Separating and Paying Interest on Debt

When a company takes on long-term debt, which means debt to be paid over more than 12 months, then the debt must be separated into current and long-term debt. The current debt will be the amount of cash that must be paid during the current year, which will include both interest and principal payments. Any amount remaining would be long-term debt.

You would need to ask your bank for an amortization chart in order to determine how much of each payment on the long-term debt goes toward interest and how much goes toward principal. You can also use an online calculator to get those numbers. A good online calculator can be found at `http://www.bankrate.com/brm/amortization-calculator.asp`.

Q. Using an amortization calculator, calculate the first three months of payments for a $20,000 five-year car loan at 7% and record the first payment.

A.

Payment 1	$279.36 principal	$116.67 interest	$19,720.64 remaining balance
Payment 2	$280.99 principal	$115.04 interest	$19,439.66 remaining balance
Payment 3	$282.63 principal	$113.40 interest	$19,157.03 remaining balance

	Debit	*Credit*
Car Loan Payable	$279.36	
Interest Expense	$116.67	
Cash		$396.02

Notice how the amount paid toward principal gradually increases, while the interest gradually decreases for a long-term debt.

14. Using an amortization calculator, calculate the first three months of payments for a $300,000 30-year mortgage at 6% and record the first payment.

Solve It

15. Using an amortization calculator, calculate the first three months of payments for a $25,000 five-year car loan at 8% and record the first payment.

Solve It

Booking Interest Income

Many businesses earn interest from money in savings accounts, money market accounts or certificates of deposit or other investment vehicles. You need to record any interest earned for the business in an Interest Income account, which will appear on the Income Statement.

Luckily you shouldn't have to calculate that interest. Your bank statement will indicate the amount of interest earned.

Q. When you get the statement from the bank you find that your business account earned $25 in interest income. How would you record that transaction in the books?

A. Here is what the entry would look like:

	Debit	*Credit*
Cash	$25	
Interest Income		$25

16. When you get the statement from the bank you find that your business account earned $53 in interest income. How would you record that transaction in the books?

Solve It

Answers to Problems on Paying and Collecting Interest

1 $20,000 × .03 × 5 = $3,000

2 $5,000 × .05 × 7 = $1,750

3 Year 1 = $20,000 × .03 = $600.00
Year 2 = $20,600 × .03 = $618.00
Year 3 = $21,218 × .03 = $636.54
Year 4 = $21,854.54 × .03 = $655.64
Year 5 = $22,510.18 × .03 = $675.31

4 Year 1 = $5,000 × .06 = $300.00
Year 2 = $5,300 × .06 = $318.00
Year 3 = $5,618 × .06 = $337.08
Year 4 = $5,955.08 × .06 = $357.30
Year 5 = $6,312.38 × .06 = $378.74
Year 6 = $6,691.12 × .06 = $401.47

5 $150 × .034076 × 12 = $61.33
$150 × .124 = $18.66

You can see that with the interest compounded daily on a credit card you pay a lot more interest on your money.

6 $150 × .0452 = $6.30

7 $150 × .0452 × 12 = $81.36
$150 × .1649 = $24.74

8 $5,000 × .10 = $500 annual interest
500/12 = $41.67 monthly interest

Payment 1: $541.67; Balance $4,500

Payment 2: $4,500 × .10 = $450 annual interest; 450/12 = $37.50 monthly interest
Payment $537.50; Balance $4,000

Payment 3: $4,000 × .10 = $400 annual interest; 400/12 = $33.33 monthly interest
Payment $533.33; Balance $3,500

Payment 4: $3,500 × .10 = $350 annual interest; 350/12 = $29.16 monthly interest
Payment $529.16; Balance $3,000

Payment 5: $3,000 × .10 = $300 annual interest; 300/12 = $25 monthly interest
Payment $525; Balance $2,500

Payment 6: $2,500 × .10 = $250 annual interest; 250/12 = $20.83
Payment $520.83; Balance $2,000

9 $10,000 × .08 = $800 annual interest

800/12 = $66.67 monthly interest

Payment 1: $1,066.67; Balance $9,000

Payment 2: $9,000 × .08 = $720 annual interest; 720/12 = $60 monthly interest
Payment $1,060; Balance $8,000

Payment 3: $8,000 × .08 = $640 annual interest; 640/12 = $53.33 monthly interest
Payment $1,053.33; Balance $7,000

Payment 4: $7,000 × .08 = $560 annual interest; 560/12 = $46.67 monthly interest
Payment $1,046.67; Balance $6,000

Payment 5: $6,000 × .08 = $480 annual interest; 480/12 = $40 monthly interest
Payment $1,040; Balance $5,000

Payment 6: $5,000 × .08 = $400 annual interest; 400/12 = $33.33
Payment $1,033.33; Balance $4,000

10

	Debit	*Credit*
Credit Card Payable	$200	
Interest Expense	$36	
Cash		$236

11

	Debit	*Credit*
Interest Expense	$47	
Cash		$47

12

	Debit	*Credit*
Interest Expense	$150	
Cash		$150

13

	Debit	*Credit*
Line of Credit Payable	$500	
Interest Expense	$85	
Cash		$585
Year 1 Payment	$298.65 principal	$1,500 interest
Year 2 Payment	$300.14 principal	$1,498.51 interest
Year 3 payment	$301.65 principal	$1,497.01 interest

14

	Debit	Credit
Mortgages Payable	$298.65	
Interest Expense	$1,500	
Cash		$1,798.65
Year 1 Payment	$340.24 principal	$166.67 interest
Year 2 Payment	$342.51 principal	$164.40 interest
Year 3 payment	$344.79 principal	$162.11 interest

15

	Debit	Credit
Car Loan Payable	$340.24	
Interest Expense	$166.67	
Cash		$506.91

16 The entry would be:

	Debit	Credit
Cash	$53	
Interest Income		$53

Chapter 13

Proving Out Your Books

· ·

· ·

Most businesses count the cash on hand each day, as well as at the end of an accounting period. In addition, each of the journals must be reviewed and closed at the end of the accounting period.

In this chapter, I explain how businesses test to be sure the cash counts are accurate. I also discuss how to handle any errors that are found, as well as start the closing process and post results to the General Ledger.

Checking Cash

At the end of each month, as businesses close their books for the month, they start by checking their cash balance. In any business cash can be found in several different places — the cash registers, incoming mail (for example, checks from customers paying bills), petty cash accounts, and the business' bank accounts. Transactions involving cash can be found in the Cash Receipts Journal (cash coming into the business) and the Cash Disbursements Journal (cash going out of the business). I talk more about closing those journals in the next section called "Closing Journals".

First you need to review the cash on hand. In Chapter 8, I talk about how to prove out the cash registers. A report of the cash remaining in each register should be sent with any records of deposits from the store managers to bookkeeping. Tallying all those records will give you a total of cash on hand in the retail outlets. The closing process for any business can take a week or more. You can't even start the process until you have the reports from all the cash registers the day after the last day of the month.

In addition you need to track any other place cash is kept in the business, such as petty cash accounts. Many businesses will have several people, such as office managers, assigned to manage small petty cash accounts for paying things like postal charges or small supply needs. You also want to tally the total of cash on hand at the bank. In the section later in this chapter called "Reconciling Bank Accounts," I discuss how to prove out those totals. Finally, you need to check the mail for any payments received on the last day of the month to be sure those checks are depositd and recorded before you close the books for the month.

Once you know your cash balance you have one key piece of the puzzle that you will need to prove out the books at the end of an accounting month.

Q. True or false: When determining how much cash the business has on hand you need to look in several places including cash register receipts, bank accounts, and petty cash boxes.

A. **True.** Cash registers, bank accounts, and petty cash boxes are all places where you may find cash assets of the business. Your business may also have other locations for cash. You need to know the total cash on hand wherever it may be as you start the process of closing the books for an accounting period.

1. True or false: Cash registers are proved out every night and the totals in the cash register are reported to the bookkeeper.

Solve It

2. True or false: The bookkeeper keeps cash on hand and gives it out if needed for small purchases.

Solve It

Closing Journals

After counting the cash on hand, you next want to find out where all the cash went that was used during the accounting period. Any cash that came into the business should be tracked in the Cash Receipts Journal and any cash that was paid out of the business should be tracked in the Cash Disbursements Journal. I talk more about the importance of these journals and how to manage them in Chapter 5.

After recording the cash from the last day's receipts into the Cash Receipts Journal, you'll need to be sure all other charges have been recorded in the journal. For example, if you allow your customers to use credit cards, you need to record any customer disputes charged back by the credit card companies.

Understanding credit card fees

Every company must pay fees to the banks that process their credit card charges. These fees lower the amount you actually take into the business, so you must adjust your credit card receipts and record the fees. Possible fees include

- ✔ **Address verification service:** This service is used to verify credit card identities so you can avoid accepting fraudulent credit cards. This is particularly important if your business accepts payment from customers by telephone or by the Internet when you don't actually see the credit card being used. Banks charge a fee for every transaction verified.

- ✔ **Discount rate:** All businesses that accept credit cards must pay for the services of the bank that handles the transactions. These costs are reflected in the discount rate, which is a percentage of each transaction. The amount of this fee varies depending on the contract rates agreed to between your business and the bank that processes your credit cards. Fees usually are set based on volume of sales.

- ✔ **Secure gateway fee:** If you are selling products over the Internet, this fee secures transactions. Businesses that use this service pay for it on a monthly basis.

- ✔ **Customer support fee:** This fee is charged to companies that want customer support 24 hours a day, 365 days a year. Mail order catalogs or Internet websites that want this round-the-clock support for orders pay this fee. Sometimes companies may make arrangements for overnight support only if they accept orders internationally, so they don't need to staff their customer service centers 24 hours a day.

- ✔ **Monthly minimum fee:** All banks set a minimum per month no matter how many transactions are handled. This fee is paid even if no credit cards were used during the month. The fee is often $10 to $30 per month. Your business won't have to worry about these fees as long as enough credit card transactions are processed. For example, if you pay a 2 percent discount fee on all credit card transactions and process $500 in transactions during the month, you would pay $10. If your monthly minimum fee is $10 then you are covered and won't have to pay the minimum. But if your monthly minimum is $30 and you only generate enough transactions for $10 in fees, then you would need to pay an additional $20 for the credit card services. If your business is just starting to think about accepting credit cards, you must be certain you will generate enough business to cover the monthly minimum fee.

- ✔ **Transaction fee:** Each time you submit a credit card transaction for approval there is a transaction fee, even if the credit card is denied.

- ✔ **Equipment and software fees:** This fee is charged based on the type of equipment and software your company uses to process credit transactions. Most stores have a small machine through which a credit card is swiped. Some companies have software added to their computerized cash registers. Whichever your company uses, there is likely to be a fee for buying or leasing the equipment or software.

- ✔ **Chargeback and retrieval fees:** If a customer disputes a transaction, then you may see a chargeback to your account when you get your bill. You will need to reverse the money entered for that sale in your books.

Q. If you pay a fee for 24 hour, 365 days per year support, which fee are you paying?

a. Customer service fee

b. Monthly minimum fee

c. Transaction fee

d. Secure gateway fee

A. The answer is **a,** customer service fee.

3. If you pay a fee to secure your Internet transactions, which fee are you paying?

a. Customer service fee

b. Monthly minimum fee

c. Transaction fee

d. Secure gateway fee

Solve It

4. For each credit card transaction you must pay a percentage of that sale to the bank that processes your credit cards. This fee is called

a. Customer service fee

b. Monthly minimum fee

c. Transaction fee

d. Discount rate

Solve It

Reconciling your credit card statements

As a bookkeeper you would go nuts trying to figure out the fees individually for each credit card transaction. Instead, the bookkeeper would adjust the cash taken in from sales using adjusting journal entries. The entries would debit (which would reduce) the Sales account and credit (which would reduce) the cash account.

In most cases the actual credit sales transactions are deposited in the company's bank account on the day the sales took place. Fees charged, as well as any chargebacks, are calculated monthly and sent to the company in a bank statement. As the bookkeeper, when you get the credit card statement from the bank, you would then total the fees and enter those fees in the books. You would also enter any chargebacks.

Q. When you get the credit card statement at the end of May, you see that there are a total of $125 in fees for the month and find that one customer disputed a charge of $35. How would you make that adjustment in the Cash journals?

A. You would make two adjusting entries — one to reverse the sale recorded in the Cash Receipts Journal and one to record the fees in the Cash Disbursements Journal. The credits reduce the amount of cash in the books. The cash has already been subtracted from your bank account. So you must reconcile what's in your books with what is in your bank account.

You would make this entry in your Cash Receipts Journal to reverse the sale:

	Debit	Credit
Sales	$ 35	
Cash		$35

You would make this entry in your Cash Disbursements Journal to record the fees:

	Debit	Credit
Credit Card Fees	$125	
Cash		$125

---

5. When you get your credit card statement you find a total of $225 were charged in fees and you find three chargebacks for customer disputes totaling $165. How would you record this information in your books?

Solve It

6. When you get your credit card statement you find a total of $275 in chargebacks from customer disputes and $320 in fees. How would you record this information in your books?

Solve It

Accruing your bills

At the end of the month you're likely to get bills that you have not yet paid. If the bills represent expenses incurred during the month, you want to record those expenses so you can match cash receipts with the expenses incurred. For example, if you took an advertisement in the newspaper for a sale on May 15 and receive the bill for that advertisement on May 30th with a due date of June 10, you want to record that bill as a May expense. This is called accruing bills.

As you close the books for the month, you want to be sure that you have accrued all bills for the expenses of that month even if you haven't paid them.

Q. Suppose you advertised a store sale in the *City Journal* on May 17. The advertisement cost $500 and you receive a bill for it on May 30. You have ten days to pay the bill. Would you need to record that bill before closing the books for May? How would you record that bill in the books?

A. Since it is a May expense, you do need to record the bill before closing the books. You would record the bill by entering a debit to Advertising expenses (to increase the amount you spent on advertising for the month) and a credit to Accounts Payable (to record the liability that must be paid). Here is what the entry would look like:

	Debit	**Credit**
Advertising	$500	
Accounts Payable		$500

7. You receive a bill for $2,500 for advertising during the month of June on June 30. You won't have to pay the bill until July. When should you record the bill? How would you record the bill?

Solve It

8. You receive a bill for $375 for office supplies for the month of May on May 30. You won't have to pay the bill until June 10, but the supplies were used primarily in May. When should you record the bill? How would you record the bill?

Solve It

Reconciling Bank Accounts

One of the biggest jobs each month is reconciling your bank account to be sure it matches your Cash account and checkbook. Often the bank statement does not come in on the last day of the month, so you reconcile your bank accounts at a different time than when you are closing the books.

You've likely had to reconcile your personal account. Well reconciling a business bank account is not much different even though it likely will include a lot more transactions than your personal account. Table 13-1 shows you a common format for reconciling a bank account.

Table 13-1	Bank Reconciliation			
Transactions	*Beginning Balance*	*Deposits*	*Disbursements*	*Ending Balance*
Balance per bank statement	$	$	($)	$
Deposits in transit (those not shown on statement)		$		$
Outstanding checks (checks that haven't shown up yet)			($)	($)
Total	$	$	($)	$
Balance per checkbook or Cash in Checking (which should be the same)				$

Q. You just got your bank statement in the mail. You find your balance at the bank is $1,200 beginning balance, $4,000 in deposits, $4,300 in disbursements, and your ending balance is $900. You review the deposits and find that a deposit of $1,000 does not show on the statement. You find that checks totaling $600 have not yet cleared. The balance in your checkbook is $1,300. Does your checkbook reconcile to the bank balance?

A. Using the bank reconciliation chart, here is the answer:

Transactions	*Beginning Balance*	*Deposits*	*Disbursements*	*Ending Balance*
Balance per bank statement	$1,200	$4,000	($4,300)	$900
Deposits in transit (those not shown on statement)			$1,000	$1,000
Outstanding checks (checks that haven't shown up yet)			($600)	($600)
Total	$1,200	$5,000	($4,900)	$1,300
Balance per checkbook or Cash in Checking (which should be the same)				$1,300

The bank statement and your checkbook do reconcile.

9. You just got your bank statement in the mail. You find your balance at the bank is $1,500 beginning balance, $6,000 in deposits, $6,500 in disbursements and your ending balance is $1,000. You review the deposits and find that a deposit of $2,000 does not show on the statement. You find that checks totaling $1,700 have not yet cleared. The balance in your checkbook is $1,300. Does your checkbook reconcile to the bank balance?

Solve It

Transactions	Beginning Balance	Deposits	Disbursements	Ending Balance
Balance per bank statement	$	$	($)	$
Deposits in transit (those not shown on statement)		$		$
Outstanding checks (checks that haven't shown up yet)			($)	($)
Total	$	$	($)	$
Balance per checkbook or Cash in Checking (which should be the same)				$

10. You just got your bank statement in the mail. You find your balance at the bank is $1,800 beginning balance, $7,000 in deposits, $6,500 in disbursements and your ending balance is $2,300. You review the deposits and find that a deposit of $1,000 does not show on the statement. You find that checks totaling $2,500 have not yet cleared. The balance in your checkbook is $1,200. Does your checkbook reconcile to the bank balance?

Solve It

Transactions	Beginning Balance	Deposits	Disbursements	Ending Balance
Balance per bank statement	$	$	($)	$
Deposits in transit (those not shown on statement)		$		$
Outstanding checks (checks that haven't shown up yet)			($)	($)
Total	$	$	($)	$
Balance per checkbook or Cash in Checking (which should be the same)				$

Sometimes you will find the balance in the bank does not match the balance in your checkbook. When that happens you will need to find out why. Here are the common things to check if you find a difference in your accounts:

If the bank balance is higher than your balance, the first thing you should look for are deposits on the bank statement that are not in your Cash account or checkbook. If you do find a deposit for which you don't have an entry, you'll need to research what that deposit was for and add it appropriately to your books. For example, if you find a bank deposit of $1,500 on May 15 and in reviewing your books don't see one that day for sales, you might want to review your sales receipts for that day and see if they were recorded. If the sales weren't recorded, it's an easy fix to do a journal entry for the sales. You also may find that you missed a check you should have listed in your outstanding checks. When you add the amount of the missing checks, you may find yourself in balance. If that's the case then you don't need to make any entries to the books.

If the bank balance is lower than your balance, the first thing you should check to see is that all the checks listed by the bank are recorded in your Cash account or checkbook. You may have sent out a check that wasn't recorded properly. If that's the case then record the check and redo your reconciliation to be sure it proves out. Another possibility is that a deposit you did make does not show up on your bank statement. If that happens you'll need to find proof of the deposit and contact the bank.

If all deposits and checks are correct, you'll then need to check your math. Make sure all checks and deposits were entered correctly as well.

Once you find the error, you will need to create a journal entry to correct the books and make sure all affected accounts are adjusted.

Q. Suppose you could not reconcile your bank statement. As you reviewed the deposits you see that a deposit of $1,000 is not recorded in your books. After researching the deposit you find that the $1,000 was a payment from a Joe Smith that did not get recorded in the books. How would you record the payment?

A. You need to reduce the amount in Accounts Receivable, because the payment is not

due. You would also need to increase the cash balance because you do have additional money in the bank.

	Debit	Credit
Cash	$1,000	
Accounts Receivable		$1,000

In addition to this entry, you would also need to update the records of Joe Smith to indicate he paid his bill.

11. Suppose you could not reconcile your bank statement. As you reviewed the checks you see there is a check written for $2,500 that is not recorded in your books. As you research the check, you find it is a payment made to Olive's Office Supplies. How would you record that in the books?

Solve It

12. Suppose you could not reconcile your bank statement and you find that a deposit of $5,300 is not recorded. As you research the deposit you find the sales receipts were not recorded for May 15. How would you record that in the books?

Solve It

Posting to the Ledger

After you checked out all the cash accounts as discussed in this chapter, you can then summarize your cash journals. I show you how to summarize journals in Chapter 4. Essentially you total the journals and then prepare a summary entry that will appear in the General Ledger. Remember the General Ledger is the granddaddy of your accounting system (see Chapter 4 for more information on the General Ledger).

Suppose you summarized your Cash Receipts Journal and got these totals for the month:

Sales Credit	$100,000
Accounts Receivable Credit	$25,000
Sale of Furniture	$5,000
Cash	$130,000

What would you enter into the General Ledger accounts?

	Debit	*Credit*
Cash	$130,000	
Sales		$100,000
Accounts Receivable		$25,000
Furniture		$5,000

With this entry your Cash account would increase by $130,000. Your Sales account would increase by $100,000. Your Accounts Receivable account would decrease by $25,000 to reflect the payments by customers and the fact that the money was no longer due. Your Furniture account would decrease by $5,000 to reflect the sale of furniture and an asset you no longer have.

---

13. Suppose you summarized your Cash Receipts Journal and got these totals for the month:

Sales Credit	$150,000
Accounts Receivable Credit	$45,000
Owner's Capital	$50,000
Cash	$245,000

What would you enter into the General Ledger Accounts?

Solve It

14. Suppose you summarized your Cash Disbursements Journal and got these totals for the month:

Rent Debit	$1,500
Accounts Payable Debits	$150,000
Salaries Expenses Debits	$35,000
Credit Card Payable Debit	$5,000
Cash	$191,500

Solve It

Answers to Problems on Proving Out Your Books

1 **True.**

2 **False.** Usually small cash needs are handled using a Petty Cash fund. Usually an office manager handles this fund.

3 **D:** Secure gateway fee.

4 **D:** Discount rate

5 The entry for the Cash Disbursements Journal would be

	Debit	Credit
Credit Card Fees	$225	
Cash		$225

The entry for the Cash Receipts Journal would be

	Debit	Credit
Sales	$165	
Cash		$165

The entry for the Cash Disbursements Journal would be

	Debit	Credit
Credit Card Fees	$320	
Cash		$320

The entry for the Cash Receipts Journal would be

	Debit	Credit
Sales	$275	
Cash		$275

6 You would need to enter the bill before closing the books for the June, so the expenses would be recorded against Junes receipts. The journal entry would be

	Debit	Credit
Advertising Expense	$2,500	
Accounts Payable		$2,500

7 You would need to enter the bill before closing the books for May, so the expenses would be recorded against May's receipts. The journal entry would be

	Debit	Credit
Office Supplies Expense	$375	
Accounts Payable		$375

8 The bank statement does reconcile to the checkbook. Here is the proof:

Transactions	Beginning Balance	Deposits	Disbursements	Ending Balance
Balance per bank statement	$1,500	$6,000	($6,500)	$1,000
Deposits in transit (those not shown on statement)		$2,000		$2,000
Outstanding checks (checks that haven't shown up yet)			($1,700)	($1,700)
Total	$1,500	$8,000	($8,200)	$1,300
Balance per checkbook or Cash in Checking (which should be the same)				$1,300

9 The bank statement does not reconcile to the checkbook. There is a difference of $400. You must review the checkbook for possible errors. Here is the solution:

Transactions	Beginning Balance	Deposits	Disbursements	Ending Balance
Balance per bank statement	$1,800	$7,000	($6,500)	$2,300
Deposits in transit (those not shown on statement)		$1,000		$1,000
Outstanding checks (checks that haven't shown up yet)			($2,500)	($2,500)
Total	$1,800	$8,000	($9,000)	$800
Balance per checkbook or Cash in Checking (which should be the same)				$1,200

11 You would need to record the office supplies expense and you would need to reflect the use of cash. Here is what the journal entry would look like:

	Debit	Credit
Office Supplies Expenses	$2,500	
Cash		$2,500

12 You would need to record the sales and you would need to record the receipt of cash. Here is what the journal entry would look like:

	Debit	Credit
Cash	$5,300	
Sales		$5,300

13 Your entry into the General Ledger accounts would be

	Debit	Credit
Cash	$245,000	
Accounts Receivable		$45,000
Sales		$150,000
Owner's Capital		$50,000

14 Your entry into the General Ledger accounts would be:

	Debit	Credit
Rent	$1,500	
Accounts Payable	$150,000	
Salaries Expenses	$35,000	
Credit Card Payable	$5,000	
Cash		$191,500

Chapter 14

Checking and Correcting Your Books

. . . .

In This Chapter

▶ Testing the books

▶ Adjusting accounts

▶ Recharting

. . . .

*O*nce all the journals are closed and their information is posted to the General Ledger, the next step in the process of closing the books is to test to see if there are any errors. This is when the rubber meets the road in bookkeeping. If all double-entry transactions have been correctly entered in the books, the books will balance and the trial will be successful. Unfortunately few bookkeepers will find that the books balance on the first try.

In this chapter, I show you how to do a trial balance and how to find any errors. Then I explore how you can correct and adjust the books if necessary.

Doing a Trial Balance Worksheet

You may think that double-entry accounting, where every transaction must include at least two entries in the books — a debit and a credit, is too much work. When you start proving out the books at the end of an accounting period and try to do a trial balance, you'll see the value of this double-entry system. After putting in hundreds, or even thousands, of entries, the initial trial balance shows you how valuable the careful balancing of each transaction can be.

There are four basic steps to developing a trial balance:

1. **Prepare a worksheet with three columns: one for the account titles, one for the debits, and one for the credits.**

2. **Fill in all account titles and record their balances in the appropriate debit or credit columns.**

3. **Total the debit and credit columns.**

4. **Compare the column totals.**

Q. You have summarized all your journal entries and posted them to the General Ledger. Using your totals for each of the accounts at the end of May in the following list, prepare a trial balance:

Cash Debit	$3,000
Accounts Receivable Debit	$1,000
Inventory Debit	$1,200
Equipment Debit	$5,050
Vehicle Debit	$25,000
Furniture Debit	$5,600
Accounts Payable Credit	$2,200
Loans Payable Credit	$29,150
Owner's Capital	$5,000
Sales Credit	$20,000
Purchases Debit	$7,500
Advertising Debit	$1,625
Interest Expenses Debit	$345
Office Expenses Debit	$550
Payroll Taxes Debit	$425
Rent Expense Debit	$800
Salaries and Wages Debit	$3,500
Telephone Expenses Debit	$500
Utilities Expenses Debit	$255

A. The trial balance for May is

Account	Debit	Credit
Cash	$3,000	
Accounts Receivable	$1,000	
Inventory	$1,200	
Equipment	$5,050	
Vehicle	$25,000	
Furniture	$5,600	
Accounts Payable		$2,200
Loans Payable		$29,150
Owner's Capital		$5,000
Sales		$20,000
Purchases	$7,500	
Advertising	$1,625	
Interest Expenses	$345	
Office Expenses	$550	
Payroll Taxes	$425	
Rent Expense	$800	
Salaries and Wages	$3,500	
Telephone Expenses	$500	
Utilities Expenses	$255	
TOTALS	$56,350	$56,350

The debits equal the credits, so the trial balance is successful.

---

1. You have summarized all your journal entries and posted them to the General Ledger. Prepare a trial balance. Your totals for each of the accounts at the end of June are

Cash Debit	$2,500
Accounts Receivable Debit	$1,500
Inventory Debit	$1,000
Equipment Debit	$5,050
Vehicle Debit	$25,000
Furniture Debit	$5,600
Accounts Payable Credit	$2,000
Loans Payable Credit	$28,150
Owner's Capital	$5,000

Sales Credit	$27,000
Purchases Debit	$12,500
Advertising Debit	$2,625
Interest Expenses Debit	$345
Office Expenses Debit	$550
Payroll Taxes Debit	$425
Rent Expense Debit	$800
Salaries and Wages Debit	$3,500
Telephone Expenses Debit	$500
Utilities Expenses Debit	$255

Solve It

Account	Debit	Credit

If your debits equal your credits in the trial balance, that's a good sign, but it's not a guarantee that your books are totally free of errors. It does mean that you did successfully enter all your transactions with balanced entries. If errors have slipped through the cracks, your accountant will probably pick them up when he prepares the financial reports.

If your books don't balance when you finish the trial balance, then you need to find the errors. Always do your trial balance with a pencil, so you can easily erase and correct the account balances and recalculate the columns. There are four steps you can take to find the errors:

1. **Check your math.** First add up your columns again and keep your fingers crossed that you just made an error in calculation. That's the simplest error to find and correct.

2. **Compare your balances.** Double-check to be sure you wrote down the correct balances for all the accounts and that you put them in the correct column as a debit or credit. If you do find an error, correct it and then retotal the columns. Hopefully that will be the answer.

3. **Check your journal summaries.** If Steps 1 and 2 don't solve the problem, you're next step is to check your math from when you summed the journal entries to be sure you don't have any errors there. If you do find an error, correct your entries, correct the posts to the General Ledger, retotal the accounts involved, and put the new totals onto your trial balance worksheet. Hopefully then you will find the debits and credits in balance.

4. **Check your journal entries and General Ledger entries.** If all else fails, you will have to check your actual transaction entries. Your financial information will be useless if you can't find out why your debits don't equal your credits. As you become more used to what you should expect each month, you will be able to scan your entries and pick out accounts with balances that look questionable. Review the entries in those accounts first. For example, if you see a total in the Office Supplies account that looks unusually high or low, then recheck the transactions you recorded to that account.

Q. If you find that your accounts are not in balance when you total your debits and credits, what is the first thing you should check?

a. Your math

b. Your balances copied to the trial balance worksheet

c. Your totals in the journal summaries

d. Your original transaction entries

A. This answer is **a,** your math. That's the easiest thing to check.

2. If you check your math and verified that you entered all the numbers correctly on the trial balance, what is the next thing you must check?

a. Your math

b. Your balances copied to the trial balance worksheet.

c. Your totals in the journal summaries

d. Your original transaction entries

Solve It

3. What is your last resort, and the most time-consuming step, if you can't find the problem with your trial balance?

a. Check your math.

b. Check your balances copied to the trial balance worksheet.

c. Check your totals in the journal summaries.

d. Check your original transaction entries.

Solve It

Making Adjustments

Once you know your accounts are in balance using the trial balance, you're not done yet. You will still need to make some adjustments to the numbers to reflect use of assets that did not involve cash. There are five key adjustments you'll probably need to make:

- ✔ **Asset depreciation:** You need to recognize the use of your long-term assets. I talk more about depreciation in Chapter 11.

- ✔ **Prepaid expenses:** Some expenses, such as insurance, must be paid on an annual or semiannual basis, even though you benefit from that payment monthly. When you close the books for the month, you adjust the monthly expenses to recognize that month's use of the asset.

- ✔ **Inventory:** If you're not using a computerized inventory system that automatically updates inventory every day, you'll need to adjust your Inventory account to reflect the amount of inventory at the end of the accounting period.

- ✔ **Bad debts:** If some customers haven't paid their bills and you decide to write off their accounts as bad debts, you need to make that adjustment in the books during the closing of the accounting period.

- ✔ **Unpaid salaries and wages:** Often a pay period will involve two different months. For example you may pay employees for the last week of May during the month of June. You would prepare an adjusting entry to acknowledge those May expenses even if you haven't yet paid the cash.

Depreciation

Depreciation commonly involves a business's largest non-cash expense. Businesses depreciate most assets that they use for more than a 12-month period, such as cars, furniture, buildings, and equipment. Most small businesses record their depreciation expenses once a year when then prepare their annual reports, but some do record them monthly or quarterly. Major corporations that must report quarterly will calculate depreciation expenses on a quarterly basis. I assume an annual depreciation expense calculation in the problems below, but if you work in a business that records monthly depreciation expenses, you will need to divide the annual depreciation expense by 12. Also to keep the calculation simple for this chapter, I use the straight-line depreciation calculation. You can review the more complicated types of depreciation calculations in Chapter 11.

Q. You are preparing to close the books at the end of the year and your company owns a truck with a cost basis of $50,000 and a salvage value of $10,000. Assume a five-year useful life. How much would you record for depreciation expenses for the year? What would your adjusting entry be?

A. $50,000 – $10,000 = $40,000 amount that will be depreciated

$40,000/5 = $8,000 amount that will be depreciated each year

	Debit	*Credit*
Depreciation Expense	$8,000	
Accumulated Depreciation — Vehicles		$8,000

The depreciation expense would be shown on the Income Statement (see Chapter 16) and the Accumulated Depreciation would be shown on the Balance Sheet (see Chapter 15).

4. Your company owns a copier with a cost basis of $30,000 and $0 salvage value. Assume a useful life of five years. How much would you record for depreciation expenses for the year? What would your adjusting entry be?

Solve It

5. Your company owns a building with a cost basis of $300,000 and a salvage value of $50,000. Assume a useful life of 39 years. How much would you record for depreciation expenses for the year? What would your adjusting entry be?

Solve It

6. Your offices have furniture with a cost basis of $200,000 and a salvage value of $50,000. Assume a useful life of seven years. How much would you record for depreciation expenses for the year? What would your adjusting entry be?

Solve It

Prepaid expenses

Sometimes your company will have to pay in advance for expenses on items from which it benefits throughout the year, such as insurance or rent. When this happens you initially enter the payment as an asset called Prepaid Expenses and then allocate the expense on a monthly basis using an adjusting entry.

Q. Suppose your company pays $7,500 semiannually for insurance on all its vehicles. You are closing the books for the month of May. What adjusting entry would you need to make?

A. First calculate the monthly expense: $7,500 / 6 months = $1,250 per month

Then you would enter this adjusting entry in the books:

	Debit	**Credit**
Insurance Expense	$1,250	
Prepaid Expenses		$1,250

The Insurance Expense would be shown on the Income Statement and the Prepaid Expenses, which are an asset on the Balance Sheet, would be reduced by the credit. This reflects the using up of the Prepaid Expenses, as well as acknowledging the expenses for the month involved.

7. Suppose your company pays $10,500 semiannually for insurance on all its vehicles. You are closing the books for the month of May. What adjusting entry would you need to make?

Solve It

8. Suppose your company pays $12,000 quarterly for rent on its retail outlet. You are closing the books for the month of May. What adjusting entry would you need to make?

Solve It

Inventory

Most businesses adjust the balance of their asset account inventory at the end of each month. Some that use a computerized inventory system may do so daily. In Chapter 7, I talk more about how to manage and value your inventory. When closing the books for the month you must take these three steps to adjust your asset account inventory:

1. **Determine the inventory remaining on hand.**

2. **Set a value for that inventory.**

3. **Prepare an adjusting entry for the General Ledger that reflects the inventory remaining.**

If you do have inventory remaining, you want to reflect that asset on the Balance Sheet and you want to reduce the cost of that remaining inventory as an expense for that month. The remaining inventory will be sold the next month. If you used inventory that was purchased the previous month, you would need to adjust the Purchases Expenses to reflect the additional expenses.

Q. At the end of the month you find that you have $10,000 of inventory remaining. You started the month with $9,500. What adjusting entry would you make to the books?

You first need to calculate the difference and determine whether you ended up with additional inventory, which means you purchased inventory that was not used that month. If that is the case you would then need to prepare an adjusting entry to increase the asset inventory and you would need to decrease your Purchases Expenses because those purchases will be sold in the next month.

A. In this case, you find that you have $500 more in inventory, so this is the adjusting entry you would need to make:

	Debit	Credit
Inventory	$500	
Purchases Expense		$500

This entry would increase the Inventory account on the Balance Sheet and decrease the Purchases Expense account on the Income Statement.

9. At the end of the month you find that you have $9,000 in ending inventory. You started the month with $8,000 in inventory. What adjusting entry would you make to the books?

Solve It

10. At the end of the month you calculate your ending inventory and find that your ending inventory value is $250 more than your beginning inventory value, which means you purchased inventory during the month that was not used. What adjusting entry would you make to the books?

Solve It

Bad debts

Sometimes you have customers that just don't pay their bills. I talk more about how to keep track of your customer accounts in Chapter 8. When you close your books at the end of the month, you should always review your customer accounts. At some point you must accept the fact that some customers will never pay. Most companies will write off nonpaying customers after they are more than six months late on paying their bills as a bad debt expense. You can record bad debts by identifying specific customers that you don't think will pay or you can establish a bad debt percentage based on historical experience. For example, if you have found over the years that 5 percent of your Accounts Receivable account will not be paid, then you can write off that percentage of Accounts Receivable each month.

0. You identify six customers that are more than six months late and the total amount due from those customers is $1,500. What adjusting entry would you make to the books?

A. You would make this adjusting entry to the books:

	Debit	*Credit*
Bad Debt Expense	$1,500	
Accounts Receivable		$1,500

With this entry the Bad Debt Expense would be shown on the Income Statement and the Accounts Receivable account balance would be reduced by $1,500 thereby reducing the asset.

11. You identify six customers that are more than six months late and the total amount due from those customers is $2,000. What adjusting entry would you make to the books?

Solve It

12. Your company has determined that historically 5 percent of its Accounts Receivable never gets paid. What adjusting entry would you make to the books if your Accounts Receivable at the end of the month is $10,000?

Solve It

Unpaid salaries and wages

If your payroll period is biweekly and the last week of the month falls under the next month's payroll, you then have to record the unpaid payroll expenses. You do this entering the anticipated payroll expenses for the week into an accrual account.

Q. Your payroll for the last week of May will not be paid until June. Your salary and wages for the biweekly payroll total $6,000 on June 7. How much would you record in payroll expenses for the month of May?

A. Your first step would be to calculate the portion of the payroll that reflects payroll expenses for the month of May. Since the payroll is on June 7 reflecting a seven-day week, you can assume that half the payroll is for May and half is for June. So $3,000 would be a May expense. Here is the entry you would make:

	Debit	Credit
Payroll Expenses	$3,000	
Accrued Payroll Expenses		$3,000

When cash is used to pay the employees in June, you would then reverse this entry:

	Debit	Credit
Accrued Payroll Expenses	$3,000	
Payroll Expenses	$3,000	
Cash		$6,000

When recording this use of cash, half of the cash is used to reverse the accrual and half is used as new payroll expenses in June.

13. Your payroll for the last full week in May is $10,000, but it won't be paid until June. How would you initially enter this in the books? How would you enter it when the cash is actually paid out? Assume the first full week of June is the same amount.

Solve It

14. Your payroll for the last four days of May will not be paid until June 8. The biweekly payroll totals $5,000 and each work week is five days. How much would you record in payroll expenses for May? What would the entry be when you initially enter it into the books? What would the entry be when the cash is actually paid out?

Solve It

15. Your payroll for the last full week of March won't be paid until April 7. The total payroll for the two weeks is $8,000. How much would you record in payroll expenses for March? What would the entry be when you initially enter this transaction into the books? What would the entry be when the cash is actually paid out?

Solve It

Reworking Your Chart of Accounts

After you fully close the books for the year, you may want to make changes to your Chart of Accounts. You may find that you didn't use an account through most of the year and you want to delete it completely the next year. Or you may find that you put all Office Expenses into one account and you think you can get a better handle on managing certain expenses, such as paper or postage, by creating separate expense accounts for the next year.

As long as you are just adding an expense account and all expense accounts start with a zero at the beginning of the year, you can just add the account and notify staff of the new account and its coding numbers for the next year. You should explain to your staff what types of expenses should be charged to that expense number. If you want to delete an expense account after it has been closed for the year, you can just delete it from the Chart of Accounts and be sure to notify staff to no longer use that account. The same process is used for revenue accounts, which also start with zero balance each year.

Asset, liability and equity accounts are handled differently because their balances carry over from year to year. For example, most businesses carry a cash balance from one year to the next, as well as buildings, furniture, equipment, and other assets. The same is true for liabilities and equity. You can't just zero out the balance of a loan on which you still owe money or bills that still need to be paid. Instead you carry over the liability balances to the next year. Company owners certainly don't appreciate losing record of their investment, so you carry over the balances in equity accounts as well.

You can always add an account during the year, but you should only delete an account at the end of a year, so you don't risk creating problems with developing your financial statements. If you do decide to add an account during the year, you'll need to transfer any transactions related to the new account from the account in which they were initially entered.

0. You decide that you want to track paper expenses separately rather than lump them into the Office Supplies Expense account. You add a Paper Expense account in the middle of the year. You've already entered $5,000 in transactions related to the buying of paper. What would you need to do to start that account?

A. First you would need to establish a new account called Paper Expense to your Chart of Accounts. Then you would need to transfer the amount of transactions involving the purchases of paper from your Office Supplies Expense account to your Paper Expenses account. Here is what the transaction would look like:

	Debit	Credit
Paper Expense	$5,000	
Office Supplies Expense		$5,000

16. You decide you want to track the amount being spent on postage separately. Prior to this you were entering these transactions in the Office Expense account. You make this decision in May, five months into your accounting year. You've already entered $1,000 for postage expenses. What would you need to do to start the account in the middle of the accounting year?

Solve It

17. You decide you want to track telephone expenses separately from other utilities. Prior to this you were entering these transactions in the Utilities Expense account. You make this decision in July, but have already recorded transactions totaling $1,400 in your books. What would you need to do to start this new account in the middle of the accounting year?

Solve It

Answers to Problems on Checking and Correcting Your Books

1 Here is the completed trial balance worksheet:

Account	Debit	Credit
Cash	$2,500	
Accounts Receivable	$1,500	
Inventory	$1,000	
Equipment	$5,050	
Vehicle	$25,000	
Furniture	$5,600	
Accounts Payable		$2,000
Loans Payable		$28,150
Owner's Capital		$5,000
Sales		$27,000
Purchases	$12,500	
Advertising	$2,625	
Interest Expenses	$345	
Office Expenses	$550	
Payroll Taxes	$425	
Rent Expense	$800	
Salaries and Wages	$3,500	
Telephone Expenses	$500	
Utilities Expenses	$255	
TOTALS	$62,150	$62,150

2 **B:** Your balances copied to the trial balance worksheet

3 **D:** Check your original transaction entries

4 Annual depreciation expense = $30,000/5 = $6,000

	Debit	Credit
Depreciation expense	$6,000	
Accumulated depreciation — Office Machines		$6,000

5 Annual Depreciation Expense = ($300,000 – $50,000) / 39 = $6,410

	Debit	Credit
Depreciation expense	$6,410	
Accumulated depreciation — Buildings		$6,410

6 Annual depreciation expense = ($200,000 − $50,000)/7 = $21,429

	Debit	Credit
Depreciation expense	$21,429	
Accumulated depreciation — Buildings		$21,429

7 Monthly insurance expense = $10,500/6 = $1,750

	Debit	Credit
Insurance expenses	$1,750	
Prepaid expenses		$1,750

Since insurance is paid semiannual, each payment includes six months.

8 Monthly rent expense = $12,000/3 = $4,000

	Debit	Credit
Rent Expenses	$4,000	
Prepaid Expenses		$4,000

9 You ended the month with $1,000 more inventory than you started the month. So you need to increase the inventory on hand by $1,000 and decrease the Purchases expense by $1,000 since some of the inventory purchased will not be used until the next month. The entry would be

	Debit	Credit
Inventory	$1,000	
Purchases		$1,000

10 Your entry would be:

	Debit	Credit
Purchases	$250	
Inventory		$250

This entry would decrease the amount of the Purchases expenses because you purchased some of the inventory which was not used.

11 Your entry would be

	Debit	Credit
Bad Debt Expense	$2,000	
Accounts Receivable		$2,000

12 First you would need to calculate the amount of the bad debt expense:

Bad debt expense = $10,000 × .05 = $500

Your entry would be

	Debit	Credit
Bad debt expense	$500	
Accounts receivable		$500

13 Your entry initially would be

	Debit	Credit
Payroll Expenses	$10,000	
Accrued Payroll Expenses		$10,000

Your entry when you actually pay out the cash would be

	Debit	Credit
Payroll Expenses	$10,000	
Accrued Payroll Expenses	$10,000	
Cash		$20,000

14 First you would need to calculate the per day payroll amount:

$5,000/10 = $500 per day

Four days of payroll = $2,000 for May payroll expense

Six days of payroll = $3,000 for June payroll expense

Your entry initially would be

	Debit	Credit
Payroll Expenses	$2,000	
Accrued Payroll Expenses		$2,000

Your entry when you actually pay out the cash would be

	Debit	Credit
Payroll Expenses	$3,000	
Accrued Payroll Expenses	$2,000	
Cash	$5,000	

15 First you need to calculate the payroll per week:

$8000/2 = $4,000

Your entry initially would be

	Debit	Credit
Payroll Expenses	$4,000	
Accrued Payroll Expenses		$4,000

Your entry when you actually pay out the cash would be

	Debit	Credit
Payroll Expenses	$4,000	
Accrued Payroll Expenses	$4,000	
Cash		$8,000

16 First you would need to establish a new account called Postage Expenses to your Chart of Accounts. Then you would need to transfer the amount of transactions involving the payment of postage from your Office Expenses account to your new Postage Expenses account. Here is what the transaction would look like:

	Debit	Credit
Postage Expense	$1,000	
Office Expense		$1,000

17 First you would need to establish a new account called Telephone Expenses to your Chart of Accounts. Then you would need to transfer the amount of transactions involving the payment of telephone bills from your Utilities Expenses account to your Telephone Expenses account. Here is what the transaction would look like:

	Debit	Credit
Telephone Expenses	$1,400	
Utilities Expenses		$1,400

Part V
Putting on Your Best Financial Face

The 5th Wave   By Rich Tennant

Corporation? Nope. Limited Partnership? Not hardly. Ahh — Soooul Proprietor.

TAX RETURN

In this part . . .

*N*ow you're ready to show off all your hard work keeping the books and find out whether or not your business made a profit. You'll learn how you use all the information you collected throughout the accounting period to prepare financial reports that give investors, lenders, vendors, government agencies and your employees, an idea about how well your company did during the month, the quarter or the year.

I also explore business ownership structures and the reports you must file with the IRS. Finally I talk about how you close out the books at year-end and get ready for the next year.

Chapter 15

Showing Everything's in Balance

· ·

· ·

After all the books are closed, it's time to prepare the financial results for the public, including governmental agencies, financial institutions, vendors, and investors. In this chapter you'll explore the key parts of a Balance Sheet, which shows what your business owns and what it owes as of a particular date, as well as how much the owners have invested in the company.

Exploring the Balance Sheet

You get a snapshot of what the business owns (its assets) and what the business owes (its liabilities or debts) when you read the Balance Sheet. You also find out how much equity owners of the business hold. It's called the Balance Sheet because it shows your accounts are in balance based on this key accounting equation:

Assets = Liabilities + Equity

One column of the Balance Sheet totals the Assets and the second column totals the liabilities and then totals the equity separately. The total of the liabilities and the equity should equal the total of the asset column.

Gathering the Numbers

Your first step in preparing the Balance Sheet will be to find all the numbers. If you've set up your Chart of Accounts properly, you should find the key accounts are at the top of the list. These include

Cash

Accounts Receivable

Inventory

Equipment

Vehicles

Furniture

Accounts Payable

Loans Payable

Owner's Capital

You'll likely have a lot more accounts. You want to make a list of all your asset, liability, and equity accounts with their balances. If you're not sure whether something is an asset, liability, or equity account, you can review the types of accounts in Chapters 2 and 3.

0. What is the Cash account?

   a. Asset

   b. Liability

   c. Equity

   d. None of the Above

A. The answer is **a**, Asset.

---

1. What is the Furniture account?

   a. Asset

   b. Liability

   c. Equity

   d. None of the Above

Solve It

2. What is the Accounts Payable account?

   a. Asset

   b. Liability

   c. Equity

   d. None of the Above

Solve It

---

3. What is the Owner's Capital account?

   a. Asset

   b. Liability

   c. Equity

   d. None of the Above

Solve It

Once you've identified all your accounts you will need to group them into five groups:

- **Current Assets accounts:** Assets that you expect to use in the next 12 months.

- **Long-Term Assets accounts:** Assets that you expect to own for more than 12 months.

- **Current Liabilities accounts:** Liabilities that you expect to pay in the next 12 months.

- **Long-Term Liabilities accounts:** Liabilities that you will pay over more than 12 months.

- **Equity accounts:** Accounts that reflect the claims owners have against the company.

4. What type of account is the Building Account?

   a. Current Asset account

   b. Long-Term Asset account

   c. Current Liability account

   d. Long-Term Liability account

   e. Equity account

Solve It

5. What type of account is the Credit Cards Payable account?

   a. Current Asset account

   b. Long-Term Asset account

   c. Current Liability account

   d. Long-Term Liability account

   e. Equity account

Solve It

6. What type of account is the Retained Earnings account?

   a. Current Asset account

   b. Long-Term Asset account

   c. Current Liability account

   d. Long-Term Liability account

   e. Equity account

Solve It

Preparing the Statement for Prime Time

Once you've grouped your accounts, you're ready to prepare the Balance Sheet. There are three types of formats used by companies:

- ✔ **Account format:** a two-column format with assets on one side and liabilities and equity on the other side.

- ✔ **Report format:** a one column layout with assets listed first, then liabilities and then equities.

- ✔ **Financial position format:** This format is used primarily outside the U.S. and has two line items not included in the account or report format — working capital and net assets. Working capital is calculated by subtracting current liabilities from current assets to give the financial statement reader a quick check on whether the company has enough current assets to pay the bills. Net assets subtracts total liabilities from total assets to show what the company has left over for its owners.

Account format

Q. To practice preparing a Balance Sheet in the account format, use this list of accounts to prepare a Balance Sheet for the ABC Company as of the end of May 2007:

Cash	$3,000
Accounts Receivable	$1,000
Inventory	$1,200
Equipment	$5,050
Furniture	$5,600
Vehicles	$25,000
Accounts Payable	$2,200
Loans Payable	$29,150
Owners Capital	$5,000
Retained Earnings	$4,500

A. This is what the account format would look like:

Company ABC Balance Sheet; as of May 31, 2007

Current Assets		**Current Liabilities**	
Cash	$3,000	Accounts Payable	$2,200
Accounts Receivable	$1,000	Total Current Liabilities	$2,200
Inventory	$1,200	Long-Term Liabilities	
Total Current Assets	$5,200	Loans Payable	$29,150
Long-Term Assets		Total Long-Term Liabilities	$29,150
Equipment	$5,050		
Furniture	$5,600	**Equity**	
Vehicles	$25,000	Owner's Capital	$ 5,000
Total Long-Term Assets	$35,650	Retained Earnings	$4,500
		Total Equity	$9,500
Total Assets	$40,850	Total Liabilities and Equity	$40,850

7. To practice preparing a Balance Sheet in the account format, use this list of accounts to prepare a Balance Sheet for the Abba Company as of the end of May 2007:

Cash	$5,000
Accounts Receivable	$2,000
Inventory	$10,500
Equipment	$12,000
Furniture	$7,800
Building	$300,000
Accounts Payable	$5,200
Loans Payable	$250,000
Owners Capital	$52,000
Retained Earnings	$30,100

Solve It

Report format

0. To practice preparing a Balance Sheet in the report format, use this list of accounts to prepare a Balance Sheet for the ABC Company as of the end of May 2007:

Cash	$3,000
Accounts Receivable	$1,000
Inventory	$1,200
Equipment	$5,050
Furniture	$5,600
Vehicles	$25,000
Accounts Payable	$2,200
Loans Payable	$29,150
Owners Capital	$5,000
Retained Earnings	$4,500

A. This is what the report format would look like:

Company ABC Balance Sheet; as of May 31, 2007

Current Assets

Cash	$3,000
Accounts Receivable	$1,000
Inventory	$1,200
Total Current Assets	$5,200
Long-Term Assets	
Equipment	$5,050
Furniture	$5,600
Vehicles	$25,000
Total Long-Term Assets	$35,650
Total Assets	$40,850

Current Liabilities

Accounts Payable	$2,200
Total Current Liabilities	$2,200

Long-Term Liabilities

Loans Payable	$29,150
Total Long-Term Liabilities	$29,150

Equity

Owner's Capital	$5,000
Retained Earnings	$4,500
Total Equity	$9,500
Total Liabilities and Equity	$40,850

8. To practice preparing a Balance Sheet in the report format, use this list of accounts to prepare a Balance Sheet for the Abba Company as of the end of May 2007:

Cash	$5,000
Accounts Receivable	$2,000
Inventory	$10,500
Equipment	$12,000
Furniture	$7,800
Building	$300,000
Accounts Payable	$5,200
Loans Payable	$250,000
Owners Capital	$52,000
Retained Earnings	$30,100

Solve It

Financial position format

0. To practice preparing a Balance Sheet in the financial position format, use this list of accounts to prepare a Balance Sheet for the ABC Company as of the end of May 2007:

Cash	$3,000
Accounts Receivable	$1,000
Inventory	$1,200
Equipment	$5,050
Furniture	$5,600
Vehicles	$25,000
Accounts Payable	$2,200
Loans Payable	$29,150
Owners Capital	$5,000
Retained Earnings	$4,500

A. This is what the financial position format would look like:

Company ABC Balance Sheet; as of May 31, 2007

Current Assets

Cash	$3,000
Accounts Receivable	$1,000
Inventory	$1,200
Total Current Assets	$5,200

Current Liabilities

Accounts Payable	$2,200
Total Current Liabilities	$2,200
Working Capital	$3,000

Noncurrent Assets

Equipment	$5,050
Furniture	$5,600
Vehicles	$25,000
Plus Noncurrent Assets	$35,650
Total Assets Less Current Liabilities	$38,650

Long-Term Liabilities

Loans Payable	$29,150
Less Long-Term Liabilities	$29,150
Net Assets	$9,500

9. To practice preparing a Balance Sheet in the financial position format, use this list of accounts to prepare a Balance Sheet for the Abba Company as of the end of May 2007:

Cash	$5,000
Accounts Receivable	$2,000
Inventory	$10,500
Equipment	$12,000
Furniture	$7,800
Building	$300,000
Accounts Payable	$5,200
Loans Payable	$250,000
Owners Capital	$52,000
Retained Earnings	$30,100

Solve It

Working with Your Balance Sheet Numbers

Every business person wants to know how he looks to the outside world and whether his company will look good to the banks or vendors from whom he may want to borrow money. If he's looking to raise additional cash for the business, he also wants to know how the numbers look to potential investors. There are three key ratios that financial institutions and investors use to find out the financial stability of a company based on the Balance Sheet numbers — current ratio, acid test ratio, and debt to equity ratio.

Current ratio

This ratio compares your current assets to your current liabilities. It provides a quick glimpse of your company's ablitity to pay its bills.

The formual for calculating this ratio is:

Current assets/Current liabilites = Current ratio

0. Suppose your Balance Sheet shows that your current assets equaled $52,000 and your current liabilities equaled $22,000. What would your current ratio be?

A. Here is how you would calculate the current ratio:

$52,000/$22,000 = 2.36

So is that number good or bad? Lenders usually look for a current ratio of 1.2 to 2, so a financial institution would consider a current ratio of 2.36 a good sign. A current ratio under 1 could be considered a sign of trouble because it indicates the company doesn't have enough cash to pay it's current bills. A current ratio over 2 may indicate that you are not investing your assets as well as you could. For example, if your company is holding a lot of cash, you may want to consider investing that money in some long-term assets such as additional equipment that you need to help grow the business.

10. Suppose your Balance Sheet shows that your current assets equaled $22,000 and your current liabilities equaled $52,000. What would your current ratio be? Is that a good or bad sign to lenders?

Solve It

11. Suppose your Balance Sheet shows that your current assets equaled $32,000 and your current liabilities equaled $34,000. What would your current ratio be? Is that a good or bad sign to lenders?

Solve It

12. Suppose your Balance Sheet shows that your current assets equaled $45,000 and your current liabilities equaled $37,000. What would your current ratio be? Is that a good or bad sign to lenders?

Solve It

Acid test (quick) ratio

The acid test ratio is a stricter test of your company's ability to pay its bills. The acid test ratio only includes the value of your cash accounts, Accounts Receivable and Marketable Securities. The value of your inventory is not included in this calculation because inventory may or may not be able to be converted to cash quickly (sold to customers in the matter of a few days). In an economic downturn it could take a while to sell your inventory. Many lenders do prefer using the acid test ratio to determine whether or not to loan your money.

Calculating the acid test ratio is a two step process:

1. **Determine your quick assets:**

   Cash + Accounts Receivable + Marketable Securities = Quick assets

2. **Calculate your acid test ratio:**

   Quick assets/Current liabilities = Acid test ratio

EXAMPLE

Q. Suppose your Balance Sheet shows that your Cash equaled $20,000, your Accounts Receivable equaled $12,000 and your Marketable Securities equaled $10,000, and your current liabilities equaled $22,000. What would your current ratio be?

A. Here is how you would calculate the current ratio:

First calculate your quick assets:

$20,000 + $12,000 + $10,000 = $42,000

Next calculate your quick ratio:

$42,000/$22,000 = 1.91

So is that number good or bad? Lenders usually look for a acid test ratio of around 1 for a company to be considerd in good condition. So an acid test ratio of 1.91 is a good sign. A current ratio under 1 could be considered a sign of trouble because it indicates the company may have to sell some of its marketable securities or take on more debt to pay its bills until it can sell some inventory.

13. Suppose your Balance Sheet shows that your Cash account equaled $5,000, your Accounts Receivable account equaled $20,000 and your Marketable Securities account equaled $10,000. Your current liabilities equaled $52,000. What would your acid test ratio be? Is that a good or bad sign to lenders?

Solve It

14. Suppose your Balance Sheet shows that your Cash account equaled $10,000, your Accounts Receivable equaled $12,000 and your Marketable Securities equaled $10,000. Your current liabilities equaled $34,000. What would your acid test ratio be? Is that a good or bad sign to lenders?

Solve It

15. Suppose your Balance Sheet shows that your Cash account equaled $15,000, your Accounts Receivable equaled $17,000 and your Marketable Securities equaled $8,000. Your current liabilities equaled $37,000. What would your acid test ratio be? Is that a good or bad sign to lenders?

Solve It

Debt-to-equity ratio

Before a business owner should even approach a lender for an additional loan, he should always check out his debt condition. One common ratio used for this purpose is the debt-to-equity ratio. This ratio compares what a business owes to what a business owns.

Calculating the debt to equity ratio is a two-step process:

1. **Calculate your total debt:**

   Current liabilities + Long-term liabilities = Total debt

2. **Calculate your debt-to-equity ratio:**

   Total debt/Equity = Debt-to-equity ratio

Q. Suppose a business's current liabilities were $22,000 and its long-term liabilities were $75,000. The owner's equity in the company totaled $67,000. What would the debt-to-equity ratio be? Is this a good or bad sign for investors?

A. First calculate the total debt:

$22,000 + $75,000 = $97,000

Next calculate the debt to equity ratio:

$97,000/$67,000 = 1.44

This debt-to-equity ratio over 1 would be a bad sign. Banks prefer the debt-to-equity ratio to be close to one. A company with a debt-to-equity ratio over 1 indicates that the owner's do not have enough invested in the company. A debt-to-equity ratio of less than 1 would not be a problem for a lender.

16. Suppose a business's current liabilites were $2,200 and its long-term liabilities were $35,000. The owner's equity in the company totaled $12,500. What would the debt to equity ratio be? Is this a good or bad sign?

Solve It

17. Suppose a business's current liabilites were $5,700 and its long-term liabilities were $35,000. The owner's equity in the company totaled $42,000. What would the debt to equity ratio be? Is this a good or bad sign?

Solve It

18. Suppose a business's current liabilites were $6,500 and its long-term liabilities were $150,000. The owner's equity in the company totaled $175,000. What would the debt to equity ratio be? Is this a good or bad sign?

Solve It

Answers to Problems on Showing Everything's in Balance

1 **A:** Asset

2 **B:** Liability

3 **C:** Equity

4 **B.** Long-Term Asset account

5 **C:** Current Liability account

6 **E:** Equity. Retained earnings tracks the earnings that are reinvested in the business each year and are part of the owner's equity in the company.

7 Here is what the account format would look like:

Abba Company Balance Sheet; as of May 31, 2007

Current Assets		Current Liabilities	
Cash	$5,000	Accounts Payable	$5,200
Accounts Receivable	$2,000	Total Current Liabilities	$5,200
Inventory	$10,500	Long-Term Liabilities	
Total Current Assets	$17,500	Loans Payable	$250,000
Long-Term Assets		Total Long-Term Liabilities	$250,000
Equipment	$12,000	**Equity**	
Furniture	$7,800	Owner's Capital	$52,000
Building	$300,000	Retained Earnings	$30,100
Total Long-Term Assets	$319,800	Total Equity	$82,100
Total Assets	$337,300	Total Liabilities and Equity	$337,300

8 Here is what the report format would look like:

Abba Company Balance Sheet; as of May 31, 2007

Current Assets

Cash	$5,000
Acounts Receivable	$2,000
Inventory	$10,500
Total Current Assets	$17,500

Long-Term Assets

Equipment	$12,000
Furniture	$7,800
Building	$300,000
Total Long-Term Assets	$319,800

Total Assets	$337,300
Current Liabilities	
Accounts Payable	$5,200
Total Current Liabilities	$5,200
Long-Term Liabilities	
Loans Payables	$250,000
Total Long-Term Liabilities	$250,000
Equity	
Owner's Capital	$52,000
Retained Earnings	$30,100
Total Equity	$82,100
Total Liabilities and Equity	$337,300

9 Here is what the financial position format would look like:

Abba Company Balance Sheet; as of May 31, 2007

Current Assets	
Cash	$5,000
Accounts Receivable	$2,000
Inventory	$10,500
Total Current Assets	$17,500
Current Liabilities	
Accounts Payable	$5,200
Total Current Liabilities	$5,200
Working Capital	$12,300
Noncurrent Assets	
Equipment	$12,000
Furniture	$7,800
Buildings	$300,000
Plus Noncurrent Assets	$319,800
Total Assets Less Current Liabilities	$332,100
Long-Term Liabilities	
Loans Payable	$250,000
Less Long-Term Liabilities	$250,000
Net Assets	$82,100

10 Calculate the current ratio:

$22,000/$52,000 = .42

This ratio is considerably below 1.2, so it would be considered a very bad sign. A ratio this low would indicate that a company may have trouble paying its bills because its current liabilites are considerably higher than the money the company has on hand in current assets.

11 Calculate the current ratio:

$32,000/$34,000 = .94

The current ratio is slightly below the preferred minimum of 1.2, which would be considered a bad sign. A financial institution may loan money to this company, but consider it a higher risk. A company with this current ratio would pay higher interest rates than one in the 1.2 to 2 current ratio preferred range.

12 Calculate the current ratio:

$45,000/$37,000 = 1.22

The current ratio is at 1.22, so it would be considerd a good sign and the company probably would not have difficulty borrowing money.

13 First you would calculate your quick assets:

$5,000 + $20,000 + $10,000 = $35,000

Then you would calculate your acid test ratio:

$35,000/$52,000 = .67

An acid test ratio of under 1 would be considered a bad sign. A company with this ratio would have a difficult time getting loans from a financial institution.

14 First you would calculate your quick assets:

$10,000 + $12,000 + $10,000 = $32,000

Then you would calculate your acid test ratio:

$32,000/$34,000 = .94

An acid test ratio of under 1 would be considered a bad sign. Since this company's acid test ratio is close to one it could probably get a loan, but would have to pay a higher interest rate because it would be considered a higher risk.

15 First you would calculate your quick assets:

$15,000 + $17,000 + $8,000 = $40,000

Then you would calculate your acid test ratio:

$40,000/$37,000 = 1.08

An acid test ratio of over 1 would be considered a good sign. A company with this ratio would probably be able to get loans from a financial institution without difficulty.

16 First you would calculate your total debt:

$2,200 + $35,000 = $37,200

Then you would calculate your debt-to-equity ratio:

$37,200/$12,500 = 2.98

A debt-to-equity ratio of over 1 would be considered a bad sign. A company with this ratio would probably be able not be able to get loans from a financial institution until the owners put more money into the business from other sources, such as family and friends or a private investor.

17 First you would calculate your total debt:

$5,700 + $35,000 = $40,700

Then you would calculate your debt-to-equity ratio:

$40,700/$42,000 = .97

A debt-to-equity ratio near 1 would be considered a good sign. A company with this ratio would probably be able to get loans from a financial institution, but the institution may require additional funds from the owner or investors as well if the company is applying for a large unsecured loan. A loan secured with assets, such as a mortgage, would not be a problem.

18 First you would calculate your total debt:

$6,500 + $150,000 = $156,500

Then you would calculate your debt to equity ratio:

$156,500/$175,000 = .89

A debt-to-equity ratio of under 1 would be considered a good sign. A company with this ratio would probably be able to get loans from a financial institution without any problems.

Chapter 16

Proving Your Profits

● ●

● ●

*E*very business person wants to know whether or not they made a profit. The Income Statement gives you the information you need to calculate a business' profit or loss for the accounting period.

In this chapter you will review the parts of an Income Statement and how it is developed. You'll then be given the opportunity to practice developing an income statement and analyzing its results.

Exploring the Income Statement

An Income Statement summarizes all the sales activities, costs incurred to produce those sales, and the expenses incurred to run the business. After reviewing these numbers a business discovers its bottom line during the accounting period being reported in the Income Statement. With this statement you can answer the crucial question — did I make a profit?

When preparing an Income Statement, the normal practice is to show three accounting periods, which can include a month, a quarter, a year, or some other period of time that makes sense for your business. For example, if you are showing the results for the year 2006, you would also include results for the years 2005 and 2004 on the Income Statement you prepare.

There are five key parts of an Income Statement:

> ✔ **Sales or Revenue:** The top line of any Income Statement shows the total sales or revenues collected during the accounting period being reported.

> ✔ **Cost of Goods Sold:** This line item shows the amount you spent to purchase the products you sold or the costs you incurred to provide the services you offer.

> ✔ **Gross Profit:** This line shows how much profit a business makes from its sales before including the overall expenses of running the business. This is calculated by subtracting Cost of Goods Sold from Sales or Revenue.

> ✔ **Operating Expenses:** The line items in this section of the Income Statement will show how much was spent when operating the business, which includes advertising, administrative expenses, rent, utilities, and any other expenses you incurred to run the business.

> ✔ **Net Income or Loss:** This is the bottom line of the Income Statement. When you subtract your operating expenses from your Gross Profit you will know whether or not the business made a profit.

0. Your Salaries and Wages account shows you paid out $5,000 in salaries and wages during the accounting period. What section of the Income Statement would include that information?

  a. Sales or Revenue

  b. Cost of Goods Sold

  c. Gross Profit

  d. Operating Expenses

  e. Net Income or Loss

A. The answer would be **d,** Operating Expenses. Salaries and wages are always considered an operating expense. While some of those salaries may have been paid to people involved in selling your products, Cost of Goods Sold only involves the expenses that can be directly linked to a product sold, such as the purchase of goods or the delivery of those goods.

1. Your Purchases account shows you purchased $10,000 worth of paper goods to be sold during the accounting period. In which section of the Income Statement would you include that account?

  a. Sales or Revenue

  b. Cost of Goods Sold

  c. Gross Profit

  d. Operating Expenses

  e. Net Income or Loss

Solve It

2. Your Telephone Expenses account shows you paid a total of $2,000 for your company's telephones during the accounting period. In which section of the Income Statement would you show that account?

  a. Sales or Revenue

  b. Cost of Goods Sold

  c. Gross Profit

  d. Operating Expenses

  e. Net Income or Loss

Solve It

3. Your Sales Discounts account shows you offered customers a total of $1,500 in discounts during the accounting period. In which section of the Income Statement would you put that information?

  a. Sales or Revenue

  b. Cost of Goods Sold

  c. Gross Profit

  d. Operating Expenses

  e. Net Income or Loss

Solve It

Formatting the Income Statement

Businesses use two different formats for their Income Statements — the single-step and the multi-step formats. Both formats contain the same information, but they look a bit different. The single-step format groups all accounts into two categories — revenue and expenses. The multi-step format divides the Income Statement into several sections and gives the reader some key subtotals not shown in the more basic single-step format including Gross Profit, Operating Expenses (separated from Costs of Goods Sold), and operating income. If the company earns income or incurs expenses from sources other than its primary business activities, such as interest income, you would set up a separate section of the Income Statement for Other Income or Expenses.

Q. Using these totals from the accounts, prepare two Income Statements — one is a single-step format and one in a multi-step format:

Net Sales	$10,000
Interest Income	$200
Cost of Goods Sold	$5,000
Advertising	$700
Salaries	$1,200
Supplies	$1,500
Interest Expenses	$500
Depreciation	$500

A. Here is what the single-step format Income Statement would look like:

Revenues

Revenues	$10,000
Interest	$200
Total Revenue	$10,200

Expenses

Costs of Goods Sold	$5,000
Advertising	$700
Salaries	$1,200
Supplies	$1,500
Interest Expenses	$500
Depreciation	$500
Total Expenses	$9,400
Net Income	*$800*

Here is what the multi-step format Income Statement would look like:

Revenues

Sales	$10,000
Cost of Goods Sold	$5,000
Gross Profit	$5,000

Operating Expenses

Advertising	$700
Salaries	$1,200
Supplies	$1,500
Interest Expenses	$500
Depreciation	$500
Total Operating Expenses	$4,400
Operating Income	$600

Other Income

Interest Income	$200
Net Income	$800

4. Using these totals from the accounts, prepare an Income Statement using the single-step format:

Net Sales	$50,000
Interest Income	$1,200
Cost of Goods Sold	$20,000
Advertising	$3,000
Salaries	$5,000
Supplies	$2,500
Interest Expenses	$1,300
Depreciation	$1,500

Solve It

5. Using the account totals from Question 4, prepare an Income Statement using the multi-step format:

Solve It

Preparing the Numbers

You may be wondering how you find the numbers for your Income Statement. You'll find those in your General Ledger (Chapter 4). If you're not sure which accounts belong on the Income Statement, I summarize the Income Statement accounts in Chapter 3 where I discuss setting up your Chart of Accounts.

Net Sales

Most Income Statements only list Net Sales in their revenue section and don't include all the accounts used to calculate those Net Sales. The key accounts used in calculating Net Sales include

- **Sales of Goods or Services:** Totals all the money the company earned selling its products, services, or both in this account.
- **Sales Discounts:** Totals any discounts you offered to customers that reduced the full price of merchandise.
- **Sales Returns:** Totals all returns from customers.

To calculate Net Sales you subtract any Sales Discounts or Sales Returns from your Total Sales (also known as Gross Sales).

Q. Looking at your accounts you find you have the following balances at the end of an accounting period:

Sales of Goods	$20,000
Sales Discounts	$2,000
Sales Returns	$1,500

Calculate your Net Sales.

A.

Sales of Goods Sold	$20,000
Sales Discounts	(2,000)
Sales Returns	(1,500)
Net Sales	$16,500

6. Looking at your accounts you find you have the following balances at the end of an accounting period:

Sales of Goods	$30,000
Sales Discounts	$4,500
Sales Returns	$2,700

Calculate your Net Sales.

Solve It

7. Looking at your accounts you find you have the following balances at the end of an accounting period:

Sales of Goods	$40,000
Sales Discounts	$6,000
Sales Returns	$2,500

Calculate your Net Sales.

Solve It

Cost of Goods Sold

You also must calculate your Cost of Goods Sold using several different accounts. While the primary account in which you track the costs incurred in buying the products you plan to sell is Purchases, not everything you purchased will be sold during the accounting period for which you are preparing the Income Statement. The Cost of Goods Sold number will reflect only those products you actually sold.

Q. Suppose you started the month of May with $100 of Inventory on hand. You purchased $1,000 of inventory during May and you have $200 of inventory left to sell at the end of May. You are preparing an Income Statement for the month of May. What would your Cost of Goods Sold be for the month of May?

A. Your Cost of Goods Sold for the month of May would be

Beginning Inventory	$100
+ Purchases	$1,000
Goods Available for Sale	$1,100
– Ending Inventory	$200
Cost of Goods Sold	$900

8. Suppose you started the month of June with $200 of Inventory on hand. You purchased $2,000 of inventory during June and you have $500 of inventory left to sell at the end of June. You are preparing an Income Statement for the month of June. What would your Cost of Goods Sold be for the month of June?

Solve It

9. Suppose you started the month of July with $500 of Inventory on hand. You purchased $1,500 of inventory during July and you have $100 of inventory left to sell at the end of July. You are preparing an Income Statement for the month of July. What would your Cost of Goods Sold be for the month of July?

Solve It

Administrative and sales expenses

You don't need to do any calculations after you total your other expense accounts. You would just list the total balance in each account on the Income Statement.

Generally you will find that your Revenue accounts carry a credit balance and your Expense accounts carry a debit balance. For more information about how debits and credits work, review Chapter 2.

Analyzing Your Income Results

Most business owners want to figure out how to improve the profits of their business. There are many different analytical tools available. In this section I introduce you to three key ratios — Return on Sales, Return on Assets, and Return on Equity. These ratios don't mean much unless you know what the common ratio is for your type of business. Check with your local chamber of commerce to find out ratios for similar local businesses. You can also order reports for your industry through BizMiner (www.bizminer.com).

Return on Sales

The Return on Sales (ROS) ratio gives you an idea of how efficiently your company runs its operations. Using this ratio you can measure how much profit your company produced per dollar of sales. You calculate ROS by dividing your net income before taxes by your net sales. If you are working for a small business owner who does not need to pay corporate taxes, you don't have to worry about taxes at all.

Q. Suppose your company had a net income of $4,500 and sales of $18,875 for the month of May, calculate the Return on Sales Ratio.

A. The Return on Sales Ratio would be

$4,500/$18,875 = 23.8%

So in this case the company made 23.8% on each dollar of sales.

10. Suppose your company had a net income of $10,595 and sales of $40,500 for the month of June, calculate the Return on Sales Ratio.

Solve It

11. Suppose your company had a net income of $13,565 and sales of $75,725 for the month of July, calculate the Return on Sales Ratio.

Solve It

Return on Assets

The Return on Assets (ROA) ratio lets you test how well you are using the company's assets to generate profits. If your company's ROA is the same or higher than other similar companies you are doing well. To calculate the ROA you divide net income by total assets. You find total assets on your balance sheet, which is discussed in Chapter 15.

Q. Your company's net income for the month of May is $4,500 and its total assets are $40,050. What is the Return of Assets ratio?

A. The Return on Assets ratio is:

$4,500/$40,050 = 11.2%

This means your company made 11.2% profit on each dollar of assets it held. The ROA ratio can vary greatly depending on industries. It can be as low as 5% for manufacturing industries that must spend a lot on equipment and factories, or as high as 20% or higher for service industries that don't need to spend as much on their assets.

12. Your company's net income for the month of May is $5,300 and its total assets are $75,040. What is the Return of Assets ratio?

Solve It

13. Your company's net income for the month of May is $10,700 and its total assets are $49,650. What is the Return of Assets ratio?

Solve It

Return on Equity

The Return on Equity (ROE) ratio measures how successful your company was in earning money for its owners or investors. You calculate ROE by dividing net income by shareholder's or owner's equity. You find the shareholder's or owner's equity on the Balance Sheet (Chapter 15).

Q. Your company earned a net income of $4,500 and its owner's equity is $50,500. Calculate the Return on Equity ratio.

A. The answer would be:

$4,500/$50,500 = 8.9%

So the owner's return on his investment is 8.9%.

14. Your company earned a net income of $75,750 and its owner's equity is $500,000. Calculate the Return on Equity ratio.

Solve It

15. Your company earned a net income of $52,500 and its owner's equity is $375,000. Calculate the Return on Equity ratio.

Solve It

Answers to Problems on Proving Your Profits

1 **B:** Cost of Goods Sold. You would use it as part of your calculation for Cost of Goods Sold.

2 **D:** Operating Expenses

3 **A:** Sales or Revenue. You would use it as part of your calculation for Net Sales.

4 The Income Statement using the single-step format would look like this:

Revenues

Net Sales	$50,000
Interest Income	$200
Total Revenue	$51,200

Expenses

Cost of Goods Sold	$20,000
Advertising	$3,000
Salaries	$5,000
Supplies	$2,500
Interest Expenses	$1,300
Depreciation	$1,500
Total Expenses	$33,300
Net Income	$17,900

5 The Income Statement using the multi-step format would look like this:

Revenues

Net Sales	$50,000
Cost of Goods Sold	$20,000
Gross Profit	$30,000

Operating Expenses

Advertising	$3,000
Salaries	$5,000
Supplies	$2,500
Interest Expenses	$1,300
Depreciation	$1,500
Total Operating Expenses	$13,300
Operating Income	$16,700

Other Income

Interest Income	$1,200
Net Income	$17,900

6 Net Sales would be

Sales of Goods	$30,000
Sales Discounts	(4,500)
Sales Returns	(2,700)
Net Sales	$22,800

7 Net Sales would be

Sales of Goods	$40,000
Sales Discounts	(6,000)
Sales Returns	(2,500)
Net Sales	$31,500

8 Your Cost of Goods Sold for the month of June would be

Beginning Inventory	$200
+ Purchases	$2,000
Goods Available for Sale	$2,200
– Ending Inventory	$500
Cost of Goods Sold	$1,700

9 Your Cost of Goods Sold for the month of July would be

Beginning Inventory	$500
+ Purchases	$1,500
Goods Available for Sale	$2,000
– Ending Inventory	$100
Cost of Goods Sold	$1,900

10 The Return on Sales Ratio would be

$10,595/$40,500 = 26.2%

So in this case the company made 26.2% on each dollar of sales.

11 The Return on Sales Ratio would be

$13,565/$75,725 = 17.9%

So in this case the company made 17.9% on each dollar of sales.

12 The Return on Assets ratio is

$5,300/$75,040 = 7.06%

13 The Return on Assets ratio is

$10,700/$49,650 = 21.55%

14 The answer would be

$75,750/$500,000 = 15.15%

So the owner's return on his investment is 15.15%.

15 The answer would be

$52,500/$375,000 = 14%

So the owner's return on his investment is 14%.

Chapter 17

Doing Your Business Taxes

· ·

· ·

*H*ow a business pays taxes and reports its income to the government depends upon how the business is structured. In this chapter, you will find a brief overview of business types and how taxes are handled for each type. You will also review the key concepts you need to file business tax returns for a sole proprietorship or a partnership. You will find a very brief overview of some key tax issues involved in corporate tax preparation, but corporate taxation can be a textbook in itself so I won't be discussing the forms that are filed.

Exploring Business Types

Not all businesses are the same. How a business is structured determines how that business will be taxed. Businesses come in four types — sole proprietorship, partnership, limited liability companies, and corporations.

Sole Proprietorships are businesses owned by one individual. These are the simplest form of business structure.

Partnerships are businesses owned by two or more individuals. This structure is slightly more complicated than a sole proprietorship because partners must work out key issues of how to divide the profits, how a partner can sell his share if he or she decides to leave, what will happen to a partner's share if he dies, and how the partnership will be dissolved if a partner wants to leave.

Limited Liability Companies (LLC) can be a sole proprietorship or a partnership, but the key difference is that the company has registered differently with the state to protect its owners from being held personally liable for company actions. This business type is somewhere between a sole proprietorship or partnership and a corporation. For example, many law firms and accounting firms are set up as LLCs.

Corporations are the most complex type of business. In legal matters they are held as a separate legal entity. Forming a corporation requires extensive legal filings. There are many rules for how the company must operate to satisfy government regulations. Owners of a corporation, known as shareholders or stockholders, cannot be sued personally for actions of the corporation, but there are extensive rules governing how a corporation must be run, as well as extensive reporting requirements to state and federal government entities.

For more information on how to choose a company structure for your business, visit the U.S. Small Business Administration's Small Business Planner (http://www.sba.gov/smallbusinessplanner/index.html) and click on "Choose a Structure."

Q. You decide to start your own home business. What type of business structure would be easiest for you to use in order to get started?

a. Sole Proprietorship

b. Partnership

c. Limited Liability Company

d. Corporation

A. The answer is **a,** Sole Proprietorship.

---

1. You decide to start your own home business, but want protection from being held personally liable for your business' activity. What type of business structure would you likely pick?

a. Sole Proprietorship

b. Partnership

c. Limited Liability Company

d. Corporation

Solve It

2. You and two of your friends decide to start a band and you need to pick a business structure. What type of business structure would you pick if you want to keep things as simple as possible?

a. Sole Proprietorship

b. Partnership

c. Limited Liability Company

d. Corporation

Solve It

---

3. You own a business that is a sole proprietorship and you want to seek additional cash by selling stock. How must you first structure your business?

a. Sole Proprietorship

b. Partnership

c. Limited Liability Company

d. Corporation

Solve It

Tax Reporting

Each business type must file different forms with the IRS to report their business activities and pay taxes on what the business earns. For sole proprietorships, partnerships, and LLCs the actual taxes due on the profits made by the business are paid by the owners of the business and filed as part of their personal tax returns. Corporations are taxed as a separate entity and must pay corporate taxes. In this section I discuss the forms that must be filed by each business type.

Sole proprietors

Sole proprietors don't have to file tax forms separately to report their business earnings. Instead most attach a Schedule C, Profit or Loss from Business, to their individual 1040 tax return. You can see a copy of this two page form at `http://www.irs.gov/pub/irs-pdf/f1040sc.pdf`.

In addition to paying taxes on any business profits at the same rate as your individual tax rate, you must also pay taxes for Social Security and Medicare. Sole proprietors must pay both the employer and employee portions of these taxes. When you are an employee you pay 6.2 percent for Social Security taxes and 1.45 percent for Medicare taxes. As a business owner, you also need to pay the employer's portion, which are the same percentages as an employee. So your Social Security and Medicare taxes are doubled — 12.4 percent for Social Security and 2.9 percent for Medicare.

Social Security taxes were paid on income earned up to $97,500 in 2007. If your business earns more than that, you don't have to pay Social Security taxes above that amount. The cap on earnings for the purpose of calculating Social Security taxes changes each year and is linked to the inflation rate. In October of each year the Social Security Administration announces the new earnings cap.

To calculate these taxes, you must file a Schedule SE, Self-Employment Tax. You can see a copy of this two-page form at `http://www.irs.gov/pub/irs-pdf/f1040sse.pdf`.

Q. Your business earns a net profit of $25,000, how much will you have to pay in Social Security and Medicare taxes?

A. For Social Security — $25,000 × .124 = $4340

For Medicare — $25,000 × .029 = $725

Total Social Security and Medicare taxes = $5065

4. You are a sole proprietor and your business earns a net profit of $125,000 in 2007. How much will you have to pay in Social Security and Medicare taxes?

Solve It

5. You are a sole proprietor and your business earned a net profit of $97,000. How much will you have to pay in Social Security and Medicare taxes?

Solve It

Partnerships

Partnerships do not have to pay taxes on their earnings; instead the earnings are paid by the owners of the partnership and reported on their individual returns. But, the business must file what is called an information return Schedule K-1 (Partner's Share of Income, Deductions, Credits, etc.) for each of its partners. The partners then use the information on the Schedule K-1 to complete their individual returns. You can see a copy of Schedule K-1 at http://www.irs.gov/pub/irs-pdf/f1065sk1.pdf.

Most partners will attach a Schedule E, Supplemental Income and Loss, to report the business earnings on their individual returns. You can see a copy of this form at http://www.irs.gov/pub/irs-pdf/f1040se.pdf.

Limited liability companies

How an LLC files taxes depends upon whether it is a sole proprietorship or a partnership. There are no specific federal tax forms for an LLC, since these types of companies are formed under state rules. If you are keeping the books for an LLC, you would file taxes according to the rules for a sole proprietorship or partnership. For more information on specific tax issues involving LLCs, read the IRS publication 3402, "Tax Issues for Limited Liability Companies" at http://www.irs.gov/pub/irs-pdf/p3402.pdf.

Corporations

Corporations come in two varieties S Corporation and C Corporation. An S Corporation can only be formed if it has less than 75 stockholders. All other corporations are C Corporations. If your business is set up as an S Corporation, the corporation must file informational returns but it is not taxed as a separate entity. Instead the stockholders report the earnings from the S Corporation on the same form used by partnerships, Schedule E.

C Corporations are taxed as an individual entity. Corporate tax filings are very complicated and beyond the scope of this book, but Table 17-1 shows you the corporate tax rates.

Table 17-1	C Corporation Tax Rates
Taxable Income	*C Corporation Tax Rate*
$0–$50,000	15%
$50,001–$75,000	25%
$75,001–$100,000	34%
$100,001–$335,000	39%
$335-$10,000,000	34%
$10,000,001–$15,000,000	35%
$15,000,001–$18,333,333	38%
Over $18,333,333	35%

6. Your business is formed as a sole proprietorship. What tax form or forms must you file?

   a. Schedule A

   b. Schedule B

   c. Schedule C

   d. Schedule SE

   e. Both C and D

Solve It

7. Your business is formed as a partnership. What tax form or forms must you file?

   a. Schedule A

   b. Schedule C

   c. Schedule E

   d. Schedule K-1

   e. Both C and D

Solve It

8. Your business is formed as an LLC, but you are a sole proprietor. What tax form or forms must you file?

 a. Schedule C

 b. Schedule E

 c. Schedule C and Schedule SE

 d. Schedule K-1 and Schedule E

 e. Schedule C and Schedule E

Solve It

9. You are a stockholder in an S Corporation. What tax form must you file to report the earnings from that corporation?

 a. Schedule A

 b. Schedule C

 c. Schedule E

 d. Schedule S

 e. No form must be added to the personal tax returns.

Solve It

Determining Sales Taxes

An even more complicated job for the bookkeeper than filing federal tax forms, can be keeping up with local and state tax rates. If your business operates in more than one locality or more than one state, you must pay taxes on sales that you make based on the rules in each of the localities and states in which your business is located.

This process can get very messy because you must add the sales tax to each sale based on the taxes for the locality or state in which the store is located. In order to collect taxes for the state, each state requires you to file an application to collect and report taxes even before you open the doors of your business. The Federation of Tax Administrators (www.taxadmin.org/) tracks changes in state tax rates, but depending on the rules for sales taxes in your state, you may have to adjust those rates based on county or city sales taxes.

Sales taxes are collected with each sale and tracked in a liability account called Sales Taxes Collected. Most states require you to pay sales taxes monthly and many provide for electronic transfer of the funds. I talk about how to calculate and record sales taxes when making a sale in Chapter 8.

Answers to Problems on Doing Your Business Taxes

1 **C:** Limited Liability Company. You can be sued personally if you structure your business as a sole proprietorship with the protection of a Limited Liability Company.

2 **B:** Partnership.

3 **D:** Corporation

4

Social Security taxes — $97,500 × .124	=	$12,090
Medicare taxes — $125,000 × .029	=	–$3,625
		$15,715

Remember that you only have to pay Social Security taxes up to earnings of $97,500, but there is no cap on earnings for Medicare taxes.

5

Social Security taxes — $97,000 × .124	=	$12,028
Medicare taxes — $97,000 × .029	=	$2,813
		$14,841

6 **E:** Both C and D. You will need to add Schedule C to report your business's profit and you will need to add Schedule SE to report Social Security and Medicare taxes obligations.

7 **E:** The business would need to file a Schedule K-1 and you would need to add a Schedule E to your personal tax returns.

8 **C:** You would need to file in the same way as a sole proprietorship. LLC does not impact how you file your federal tax returns. LLCs are state chartered.

9 **C:** You would get a statement of earnings from the S Corporation and report those earnings on a Schedule E.

Chapter 18

Getting Ready for a New Bookkeeping Year

At the end of every accounting period certain accounts are closed and others remain open. In this chapter, you will review the accounts that continue from one business cycle to the next, as well as the accounts that must be closed at the end of each cycle and started with a zero balance in the next cycle. You'll explore key decisions that must be made about customer and vendor accounts.

Finalizing the Ledger

Once you've processed all possible payments for the year and accounted for all possible income, reviewed all your accounts, balanced out your books, and prepared the financial statements for the accounting period, it's time to finalize your General Ledger and get ready for a new year. Some accounts will carry over their balances into the new year (Balance Sheet accounts) and others will start with a zero balance (Income Statement accounts).

Closing Income Statement accounts

Once you're sure you've made any needed corrections or adjustments that were identified when preparing your trial balance (Chapter 14) and you've collected the information needed from those accounts for your financial statements, you can then zero out the balances of all the Income Statement accounts. This will include all revenue, cost of goods sold, and expense accounts.

You don't throw away the accounting information for the prior accounting period. You just start new pages in your journals and General Ledger accounts with a zero balance for the new accounting period.

If you're using a computerized accounting system, follow the procedures for closing the accounting period. The accounting system will archive the data for the accounting period and zero out the accounts during the closing process.

Carrying over Balance Sheet accounts

Balance Sheet accounts never get zeroed out. All these accounts will carry their balance into the next year. You still have the underlying assets, such as cash in your bank accounts, furniture in your stores or buildings you own, so you don't want to zero out their values. You still owe your creditors and will need to pay any debts either during the next accounting period or during some future accounting period. For example, a mortgage is paid over many years and its balance would be carried over until paid off. The owners of the company certainly still own their share of the company and you must carry over details of that ownership.

Q. You are closing the books for the accounting period and have a $75,000 balance in your Sales account. What should you do with that balance?

a. Zero it out

b. Carry it over to the next accounting period

c. Start a new Sales account

d. Ignore It

A. The answer is **a**, Zero it out. All Income Statement accounts start with a zero balance in a new accounting period.

---

1. You are closing the books for the accounting period and have a $50,000 balance in your Purchasing account. What should you do with that balance?

a. Zero it out

b. Carry it over to the next accounting period

c. Start a new Sales account

d. Ignore It

Solve It

2. You are closing the books for the accounting period and have a $25,000 balance in your Cash account. What should you do with that balance?

a. Zero it out

b. Carry it over to the next accounting period

c. Start a new Cash account

d. Ignore It

Solve It

3. You are closing the books for the accounting period and have a $150,000 balance in your Loans Payable account. What should you do with that balance?

a. Zero it out

b. Carry it over to the next accounting period

c. Start a new Loans Payable account

d. Ignore It

Solve It

4. You are closing the books for the accounting period and have a $125,000 balance in your Owner's Equity account. What should you do with that balance?

a. Zero it out

b. Carry it over to the next accounting period

c. Start a new Owner's Equity account

d. Ignore It

Solve It

5. You are closing the books for the accounting period and have a $35,000 balance in your Advertising account. What should you do with that balance?

a. Zero it out

b. Carry it over to the next accounting period

c. Start a new Advertising account

d. Ignore It

Solve It

Reviewing Customer Accounts

You will likely close your books on a monthly basis, but do a more extensive closing process at the end of a 12-month accounting period. During this year-end close it's a good idea to take a more critical look at your customer accounts. In Chapter 8 I discuss writing off accounts for bad debts, but at year-end it's time to take a harder look. Bad debt can be used as an expense to reduce taxes, so if you believe certain customers will never pay, it's a good idea to just write them off at year-end and not pay taxes on what otherwise would be shown as a profit for your company. Even if you're a sole proprietor, reducing net income will reduce the amount of taxes you must pay on your profits. In fact a sole proprietor can reduce not only income taxes, but also Social Security and Medicare taxes when he or she reduces net income.

Q. At the end of the year when closing the books, you find you have six customers who are more than 90 days past due. You don't expect any of the customers to pay. The customers owe a total of $1,500. What entry should you make in your books?

A. You should make this entry:

	Debit	Credit
Bad Debt	$1,500	
Accounts Receivable		$1,500

You should also reflect the write-off in each of the customer's accounts.

6. At the end of the year when closing the books, you find you have three customers who are more than 90 days past due. You don't expect any of the customers to pay. The customers owe a total of $750. What entry should you make in your books?

Solve It

Assessing Vendor Accounts

During the closing process you should also review your vendor accounts to be sure all bills related to the prior accounting period are entered into the books. If you find an unpaid bill that does reflect expenses for the period you are about to close, you should record that bill by crediting the Accounts Payable account and debiting the appropriate account.

Q. In reviewing your vendor accounts, you find that the most recent telephone bill of $135 is not paid or recorded, but it does reflect expenses incurred during the accounting period that is being closed. How should you record that in the books?

A.

	Debit	Credit
Telephone Expenses	$135	
Accounts Payable		$135

If you already completed your trial balance, you will need to adjust the numbers to reflect this missing expense.

7. In reviewing your vendor accounts, you find that your most recent electric bill totaling $235 for electricity used in the prior month was not paid or recorded, but it does reflect expenses incurred during the accounting period that is being closed. How should you record that in the books?

Solve It

Deleting Accounts

At the end of an accounting year is a good time to review all your accounts and decide whether or not you still them. If you decide you don't need an account any longer, the closing process is an ideal time to delete accounts. You should never delete an account in the middle of an accounting year. If you do find that you want to delete an account in the middle, then start a list of accounts you want to delete at the end of the year.

If an account you want to delete is an Income Statement account, then it's very easy to delete. Because you will be zeroing out all the accounts, you can just delete the account from your Chart of Accounts. If the account is a balance sheet account and it does carry a balance, you will need to move the value of the assets, liabilities, or equities to an account that will still be open. You would move the assets by making an entry in your General Ledger.

Q Suppose you want to consolidate all your vehicle asset accounts into one account at the end of the accounting year. You have an asset account called Vehicles — Trucks with a debit balance of $20,000 and an asset account called Vehicles — Cars with a debit balance of $15,000. What entry would you need to make in the general ledger to close the two vehicle accounts and start a new one just called Vehicles?

A The entry would be

	Debit	Credit
Vehicles	$35,000	
Vehicles – Trucks		$20,000
Vehicles – Cars		$15,000

8. Suppose you decide to consolidate your Credit Card Payable liability accounts into one at the end of the accounting year. You have a liability account called Credit Cards Payable– Bank One with a credit balance of $5,000 and a liability account called Credit Cards Payable – American Bank with a credit balance of $500. What entry would you make in the General Ledger to consolidate these accounts into an account called Credit Cards Payable?

Solve It

Preparing to Restart Business Cycle

The monthly closing process for any business can take a week or more as needed adjustments and corrections are made. Closing at year-end can take several weeks. Most businesses will send out notices to their employees telling them any revenues or expenses that they want entered for the current year must be in accounting by a certain cutoff date.

During the closing process, a bookkeeper will probably be working with two sets of books: one set that is being closed and a new set for the new account cycle. If you are closing the books at month-end, you may just start a new journal page for the new month. But, at year-end you would more likely have a new set of journals for the new year.

If you are using a computerized accounting system, this restart of the accounting cycle will be managed by the software program, but it is a good idea to print out a report of your year-end account data before starting the closing process in case something goes wrong. Also you should back up your data on a disc before starting the closing process in your computerized accounting system.

At year-end you will also need to make up new files for all your vendors, contractors, and customers. If you have room in your office, you will likely use one file cabinet for the current year and one for the previous year. To set up the files for the new year, you would likely box up the files from two years ago and use those drawers for the new year. For example, if you are getting ready for 2008 and have one filing cabinet with 2007 files and one with 2006 files, you would box up the 2006 files to make room for the 2008 files. In Chapter 6, I discuss record keeping and how long you must keep your files.

Answers to Problems on Getting Ready for a New Bookkeeping Year

1 **A:** Zero it out. The Purchasing account is part of the calculation for cost of goods sold. This is an Income Statement account.

2 **B:** Carry it over to the next accounting period. You certainly want to keep track of your cash. It doesn't disappear just because you enter a new accounting period. The Cash account is a Balance Sheet account, as are all asset accounts.

3 **B:** Carry it over to the next accounting period. While you might wish you could zero out a loan, unfortunately you can't and you do need to carry over the liability to the next accounting period. All liability accounts are Balance Sheet accounts.

4 **B:** Carry it over to the next accounting period. Owners certainly don't want to lose track of the amount they've invested in the company. All equity accounts (Balance Sheet accounts) are carried over to the next accounting period.

5 **A:** Zero it out. The Advertising account is an expense account and it is shown on the Income Statement. You don't carry over expenses from one accounting period to the next.

6 You should make this entry:

	Debit	*Credit*
Bad Debt	$750	
Accounts Receivable		$750

7 You should make this entry:

	Debit	*Credit*
Utility Expenses	$235	
Accounts Payable		$235

8 You should make this entry into the General Ledger:

	Debit	*Credit*
Credit Cards Payable – Bank One	$5,000	
Credit Cards Payable – American Bank	$500	
Credit Cards Payable		$5,500

Part VI
The Part of Tens

The 5th Wave   By Rich Tennant

"You ever notice how doing the books is a lot like assembling a swing set for the kids? You always end up with a few pieces left over at the end."

In this part . . .

I join in the *For Dummies* series tradition of showing you some lists of tens — key factors to maintaining your books and using the information collected. I highlight the top ten accounts you should monitor and the top ten ways to manage your business' cash using your books.

Chapter 19

Top Ten Checklist for Managing Your Cash

Many business owners think of bookkeeping as a necessary evil, but in reality if you make effective use of the data collected, bookkeeping can be your best buddy for managing your cash. The key to taking advantage of what bookkeeping has to offer is understanding the value of basic bookkeeping principles and taking advantage of the information collected. This chapter reviews the top ten ways to manage your business cash with your books.

Charting the Way

You may think that a list of accounts, called the Chart of Accounts, is not a big deal. Well that's far from the truth. The Chart of Accounts dictates how your financial data will be collected and where your transactions will be put. It's crucial to define each account carefully and determine exactly what types of transactions will go where in order to be able to use the information collected effectively. I talk more about the Chart of Accounts and how to set one up in Chapter 3.

Balancing Your Entries

Keeping your books balanced is the only way to know how your business is doing. You can never know whether your profit numbers are accurate, if your business' books don't balance. In bookkeeping, a process called double-entry bookkeeping is used to keep the books balanced. I talk more about this basic principle and how to keep the books balanced in Chapter 2.

Posting Your Transactions

In order to be able to use the information regarding your business transactions, they must be posted accurately to your accounts. If you forgot to post a transaction to your books, your reports will not reflect that financial activity. Or, if you post a transaction to your books that is not accurate, your reports using that information will be wrong. I talk more about the posting process in Chapters 4 and 5.

Tracking Customer Collections

If your business sells to customers on store credit, you certainly want to be sure your customers pay for their purchases in the future. Customer account information is collected in the Accounts Receivable account, as well as in individual records for each customer. You should review reports based on customer payment history, called aging reports, on a monthly basis to be sure customers are paying on time. You may want to cut off customers from future purchases if their accounts are past due for 90 days or more. You set the rules for store credit. I talk more about how to manage customer accounts in Chapter 8.

Paying Bills Accurately and on Time

If you want to continue getting supplies, products, and services from your vendors and contractors, you must be sure you pay them accurately and on time. You also want to be sure that you don't pay anyone twice. Payments are managed through the Accounts Payable account. You should review your payment history and be sure your are making timely and accurate payments. I talk more about managing your payments in Chapter 7.

Planning Profits

Nothing is more important to a business owner than the profits he will ultimately make. Yet many business owners don't take the time to plan their profit expectations at the beginning of each year, so they have nothing to use to gauge how well they are doing throughout the year. Take the time to develop profit expectations and a budget that will help you meet the expectations before the year starts. Then develop a series of internal financial reports using the numbers you collect in your bookkeeping system that will help you determine whether or not you are meeting your sales targets and maintaining control over your product costs and operating expenses. I talk more about sales tracking in Chapter 8, costs and expense tracking in Chapter 7, and how to determine your net profit in Chapter 15.

Comparing Budget to Actual Expenses

Keeping a careful watch on how well your budget planning reflects what is actually going on in your business can help you meet your profit goals. Take the time to develop a budget that sets your expectations for the year and then develop internal reports that give you the ability to track how closely your actual expenses match that budget. If you see any major problems, correct them as soon as possible to be sure you'll be able to meet your target profit at the end of the year. I talk about managing expenses in Chapter 7.

Comparing Sales Goals to Actual Sales

In addition to watching your expenses, you also need to be sure your actual sales match the sales goals you set at the beginning of the year. Designing an internal report that allows you to track sales goals versus actual sales gives you the ability to monitor how well your business is doing. If you find your actual sales are below expectations, the earlier in the year you correct that problem the better chance you'll have to meet those year-end goals. I talk about how to track sales in Chapter 8.

Tracking Cost Trends

It's important to know what is happening to the costs involved in purchasing the products you sell or the raw materials you use to manufacture your products. These costs trends can have a major impact on whether or not your company will earn the net income you expect. If you find the costs are trending upward, you may need to adjust the prices of the products you sell in order to meet your profit goals. I talk more about tracking cost trends in Chapter 7.

Making Pricing Decisions

Many factors must be considered when determining what price to charge your customers. You need to consider not only how much you pay to buy the product (or to manufacture the product) you sell, but you also must factor in what you pay your employees as well as other advertising and administrative expenses you incur in order to set a price. You can't set that price too high though or you may not find any customers willing to buy the product. Properly pricing your product can be a critical factor in determining whether or not your product will sell. While the numbers in your books regarding product costs and operating expenses are not the only factor in making a pricing decision, the information is critical to help you make that decision. You'll also need market research about what customers will pay for a product in addition to the product cost and operating expense data to set a price. I talk more about tracking costs and expenses in Chapter 7 and calculating profit in Chapter 16.

Chapter 20

Top Ten Accounts You Should Monitor

While each and every account has its purpose in bookkeeping, all accounts are not created equally. Some accounts are more critical than others. This chapter looks at the top ten accounts for bookkeepers.

Cash

All of a business' transactions pass through this account, which is so important that there are actually two journals used to track the transactions — the Cash Receipts Journal and the Cash Disbursements Journal. I discuss these journals in Chapter 5. As the bookkeeper it is your responsibility to be sure that all cash — whether it is coming into the business or being sent out — is handled and recorded properly.

Accounts Receivable

If your company sells its products or services to customers on store credit, then this account becomes very critical. The Accounts Receivable account tracks all money due from customers. As the bookkeeper, it's critical to keep this account up-to-date. You want to be sure that timely and accurate bills are sent to customers and that customers are paying their bills on time. I talk more about the Accounts Receivable process in Chapter 8.

Inventory

Every company must have products to sell. Those money-making products must be carefully accounted for and tracked. The bookkeeper helps with this process by keeping accurate inventory records, which are periodically tested by doing physical counts of the inventory on hand. Many stores will close their doors for a day to do a physical count of inventory. I talk more about how to manage inventory in Chapter 7.

Accounts Payable

While no one likes to send money out of the business, tracking and paying bills in Accounts Payable is critical. You certainly don't want to pay anyone twice, but you also want to be sure you do pay the bills on time or your company may no longer get the supplies, inventory, or other things that are needed to operate the business. Late paying companies are often cut off by suppliers or put on cash-only accounts, which means you must pay cash to get any supplies. You also may be able to get discounts and save money if you pay the bills early. I talk more about Accounts Payable in Chapter 7.

Loans Payable

Every company needs to purchase major items, such as equipment, vehicles, and furniture, but may not have the money to pay for it. Instead companies take long-term loans that must be paid over more than a 12-month period. In order to get the best rates for these loans, it's critical that the bookkeeper make all loan payments on time and accurately. I talk more about paying loans and interest due in Chapter 12.

Sales

No business can operate without taking in cash and most cash is taken in through the sales of the company's products or services. The Sales account tracks all incoming revenue collected from these sales. It's critical that the bookkeeper record sales in a timely and accurate manner, so the business owner knows exactly how much revenue has been collected every day. I talk more about sales in Chapter 8.

Purchases

Companies either manufacture the goods they sell or they purchase finished goods from various suppliers. Even if the goods are manufactured in house, raw materials will have to be purchased to make those goods. The Purchases account is used to track the purchase of any finished goods or raw materials. The Purchases account is a key component to calculating Cost of Goods Sold, which is subtracted from Sales to find out a company's gross profit. I talk more about the Purchases account in Chapter 7.

Payroll Expenses

You must pay employees to get them to stay around. Few people want to work for nothing. You track all money paid to employees in the Payroll Expenses account. For many businesses this can be their biggest expense. It's important for the bookkeeper to track these expenses accurately, but it's also important that all governmental reports are filed and payroll taxes are paid. I talk more about payroll obligations in Chapters 9 and 10.

Office Expenses

Another key expense that can drain a company's profits are office expenses. This includes paper, pens, paperclips, and any other supplies needed to run the office. Expenses related to office machinery also fall under this account. These expenses tend to creep up if not carefully monitored. I talk more about internal controls and record keeping in Chapter 6, including controls that can be put in place involving office expenses.

Owner's Equity

Accounts related to owner's equity will vary depending upon the type of business for which you keep the books. Many small businesses are owned by one person or a group of partners. They are not incorporated and therefore there are no shares of stock that apportion ownership. Instead money put into the business by each of the owners is tracked in Capital accounts. Any money taken out of the business will be shown in Drawing accounts. In order to be fair to all owners, it's critical that the bookkeeper carefully track all owner's equity accounts. I talk more about business structures and types of ownership in Chapter 17.

Retained Earnings

Any profit made by the company that is reinvested for growing the company is called retained earnings. These are earnings that are not paid out to company owners. This account is cumulative, which means it shows the total of earnings that have been retained since the company opened its doors. While it doesn't take a lot of time for the bookkeeper to manage this account, it's ongoing accuracy is important to investors and lenders who want to track how well the company is doing. I talk more about retained earnings in Chapter 15.

Chapter 21

Top Ten Problems You Should Practice

*T*ake the time to be certain you've mastered the key concepts of bookkeeping by practicing the problems related to these key bookkeeping concepts. This chapter highlights the key bookkeeping functions you want to be sure you can understand and can do.

Identifying Accounts and Using Double-Entry Bookkeeping

You'll find as a bookkeeper it is essential to enter transactions into the correct accounts, so you need to practice identifying what types of transactions go into what types of accounts. Plus, if you want to keep your books in balance, you must understand the basics of double-entry bookkeeping. Spend some extra time on both of these concepts by working the problems in Chapter 2.

Keeping Journals

Every financial transaction for your business will need to be entered into journals. They are the key day-to-day tracking tools for your company's financial history. Review what journals are and practice making journal entries in Chapter 5.

Paying Bills and Managing Inventory

If you don't pay your creditors, vendors, and anyone else to whom your company owes money, you won't be in business for long. You also need to keep track of what you sell, how many products you have on hand, and know how to value that inventory. You can better manage your company's outgoing cash and inventory by practicing these concepts in Chapter 7.

Tracking Sales

Keeping track of money coming into the company is the fun part. Everyone enjoys entering incoming cash. It's what keeps the company on a good financial footing. Make sure you know how to enter your company's revenues by reviewing Chapter 8 and the problems related to tracking revenues.

Testing Your Balance

After you've entered all you company's transactions you need to be sure the books are in balance (see Chapter 14). If they aren't, the financial statements you generate based on the data collected will be useless. And because any company's lenders, vendors, and owners want to know if the company finances are in balance, you need to also know how to prepare a Balance Sheet (see Chapter 15).

Reporting Income

Every business owner loves to see how much money he made. You make this possible by pulling together the accounts related to income and expenses and preparing an Income Statement (see Chapter 16).

Closing the Books and Starting Over

At the end of every accounting cycle you need to close out the books and prepare financial statements (see Chapter 13). And after closing out the books, you then have to get ready for the next bookkeeping year. You can practice the key steps of preparing for the next year by working the problems in Chapter 18.

Index

Notes

BUSINESS, CAREERS & PERSONAL FINANCE

0-7645-9847-3

0-7645-2431-3

Also available:
- Business Plans Kit For Dummies
0-7645-9794-9
- Economics For Dummies
0-7645-5726-2
- Grant Writing For Dummies
0-7645-8416-2
- Home Buying For Dummies
0-7645-5331-3
- Managing For Dummies
0-7645-1771-6
- Marketing For Dummies
0-7645-5600-2

- Personal Finance For Dummies
0-7645-2590-5*
- Resumes For Dummies
0-7645-5471-9
- Selling For Dummies
0-7645-5363-1
- Six Sigma For Dummies
0-7645-6798-5
- Small Business Kit For Dummies
0-7645-5984-2
- Starting an eBay Business For Dummies
0-7645-6924-4
- Your Dream Career For Dummies
0-7645-9795-7

HOME & BUSINESS COMPUTER BASICS

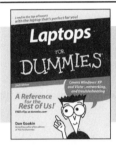

0-470-05432-8

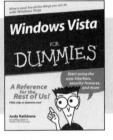

0-471-75421-8

Also available:
- Cleaning Windows Vista For Dummies
0-471-78293-9
- Excel 2007 For Dummies
0-470-03737-7
- Mac OS X Tiger For Dummies
0-7645-7675-5
- MacBook For Dummies
0-470-04859-X
- Macs For Dummies
0-470-04849-2
- Office 2007 For Dummies
0-470-00923-3

- Outlook 2007 For Dummies
0-470-03830-6
- PCs For Dummies
0-7645-8958-X
- Salesforce.com For Dummies
0-470-04893-X
- Upgrading & Fixing Laptops For Dummies
0-7645-8959-8
- Word 2007 For Dummies
0-470-03658-3
- Quicken 2007 For Dummies
0-470-04600-7

FOOD, HOME, GARDEN, HOBBIES, MUSIC & PETS

0-7645-8404-9

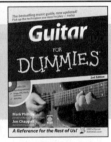

0-7645-9904-6

Also available:
- Candy Making For Dummies
0 7615 9734 5
- Card Games For Dummies
0-7645-9910-0
- Crocheting For Dummies
0-7645-4151-X
- Dog Training For Dummies
0-7645-8418-9
- Healthy Carb Cookbook For Dummies
0-7645-8476-6
- Home Maintenance For Dummies
0-7645-5215-5

- Horses For Dummies
0-7645-9797-3
- Jewelry Making & Beading For Dummies
0-7645-2571-9
- Orchids For Dummies
0-7645-6759-4
- Puppies For Dummies
0-7645-5255-4
- Rock Guitar For Dummies
0-7645-5356-9
- Sewing For Dummies
0-7645-6847-7
- Singing For Dummies
0-7645-2475-5

INTERNET & DIGITAL MEDIA

0-470-04529-9

0-470-04894-8

Also available:
- Blogging For Dummies
0-471-77084-1
- Digital Photography For Dummies
0-7645-9802-3
- Digital Photography All-in-One Desk Reference For Dummies
0-470-03743-1
- Digital SLR Cameras and Photography For Dummies
0-7645-9803-1
- eBay Business All-in-One Desk Reference For Dummies
0-7645-8438-3
- HDTV For Dummies
0-470-09673-X

- Home Entertainment PCs For Dummies
0-470-05523-5
- MySpace For Dummies
0-470-09529-6
- Search Engine Optimization For Dummies
0-471-97998-8
- Skype For Dummies
0-470-04891-3
- The Internet For Dummies
0-7645-8996-2
- Wiring Your Digital Home For Dummies
0-471-91830-X

* Separate Canadian edition also available
† Separate U.K. edition also available

SPORTS, FITNESS, PARENTING, RELIGION & SPIRITUALITY

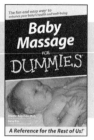

0-471-76871-5

0-7645-7841-3

Also available:

- Catholicism For Dummies
  0-7645-5391-7
- Exercise Balls For Dummies
  0-7645-5623-1
- Fitness For Dummies
  0-7645-7851-0
- Football For Dummies
  0-7645-3936-1
- Judaism For Dummies
  0-7645-5299-6
- Potty Training For Dummies
  0-7645-5417-4
- Buddhism For Dummies
  0-7645-5359-3

- Pregnancy For Dummies
  0-7645-4483-7 †
- Ten Minute Tone-Ups For Dummies
  0-7645-7207-5
- NASCAR For Dummies
  0-7645-7681-X
- Religion For Dummies
  0-7645-5264-3
- Soccer For Dummies
  0-7645-5229-5
- Women in the Bible For Dummies
  0-7645-8475-8

TRAVEL

0-7645-7749-2

0-7645-6945-7

Also available:

- Alaska For Dummies
  0-7645-7746-8
- Cruise Vacations For Dummies
  0-7645-6941-4
- England For Dummies
  0-7645-4276-1
- Europe For Dummies
  0-7645-7529-5
- Germany For Dummies
  0-7645-7823-5
- Hawaii For Dummies
  0-7645-7402-7

- Italy For Dummies
  0-7645-7386-1
- Las Vegas For Dummies
  0-7645-7382-9
- London For Dummies
  0-7645-4277-X
- Paris For Dummies
  0-7645-7630-5
- RV Vacations For Dummies
  0-7645-4442-X
- Walt Disney World & Orlando
  For Dummies
  0-7645-9660-8

GRAPHICS, DESIGN & WEB DEVELOPMENT

0-7645-8815-X

0-7645-9571-7

Also available:

- 3D Game Animation For Dummies
  0-7645-8789-7
- AutoCAD 2006 For Dummies
  0-7645-8925-3
- Building a Web Site For Dummies
  0-7645-7144-3
- Creating Web Pages For Dummies
  0-470-08030-2
- Creating Web Pages All-in-One Desk
  Reference For Dummies
  0-7645-4345-8
- Dreamweaver 8 For Dummies
  0-7645-9649-7

- InDesign CS2 For Dummies
  0-7645-9572-5
- Macromedia Flash 8 For Dummies
  0-7645-9691-8
- Photoshop CS2 and Digital
  Photography For Dummies
  0-7645-9580-6
- Photoshop Elements 4 For Dummies
  0-471-77483-9
- Syndicating Web Sites with RSS Feeds
  For Dummies
  0-7645-8848-6
- Yahoo! SiteBuilder For Dummies
  0-7645-9800-7

NETWORKING, SECURITY, PROGRAMMING & DATABASES

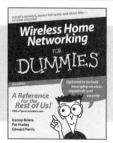

0-7645-7728-X

0-471-74940-0

Also available:

- Access 2007 For Dummies
  0-470-04612-0
- ASP.NET 2 For Dummies
  0-7645-7907-X
- C# 2005 For Dummies
  0-7645-9704-3
- Hacking For Dummies
  0-470-05235-X
- Hacking Wireless Networks
  For Dummies
  0-7645-9730-2
- Java For Dummies
  0-470-08716-1

- Microsoft SQL Server 2005 For Dummies
  0-7645-7755-7
- Networking All-in-One Desk Reference
  For Dummies
  0-7645-9939-9
- Preventing Identity Theft For Dummies
  0-7645-7336-5
- Telecom For Dummies
  0-471-77085-X
- Visual Studio 2005 All-in-One Desk
  Reference For Dummies
  0-7645-9775-2
- XML For Dummies
  0-7645-8845-1

HEALTH & SELF-HELP

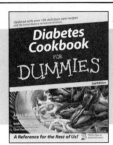
0-7645-8450-2

0-7645-4149-8

Also available:

✔Bipolar Disorder For Dummies
0-7645-8451-0
✔Chemotherapy and Radiation
For Dummies
0-7645-7832-4
✔Controlling Cholesterol For Dummies
0-7645-5440-9
✔Diabetes For Dummies
0-7645-6820-5* †
✔Divorce For Dummies
0-7645-8417-0 †

✔Fibromyalgia For Dummies
0-7645-5441-7
✔Low-Calorie Dieting For Dummies
0-7645-9905-4
✔Meditation For Dummies
0-471-77774-9
✔Osteoporosis For Dummies
0-7645-7621-6
✔Overcoming Anxiety For Dummies
0-7645-5447-6
✔Reiki For Dummies
0-7645-9907-0
✔Stress Management For Dummies
0-7645-5144-2

EDUCATION, HISTORY, REFERENCE & TEST PREPARATION

0-7645-8381-6

0-7645-9554-7

Also available:

✔The ACT For Dummies
0-7645-9652-7
✔Algebra For Dummies
0-7645-5325-9
✔Algebra Workbook For Dummies
0-7645-8467-7
✔Astronomy For Dummies
0-7645-8465-0
✔Calculus For Dummies
0-7645-2498-4
✔Chemistry For Dummies
0-7645-5430-1
✔Forensics For Dummies
0-7645-5580-4

✔Freemasons For Dummies
0-7645-9796-5
✔French For Dummies
0-7645-5193-0
✔Geometry For Dummies
0-7645-5324-0
✔Organic Chemistry I For Dummies
0-7645-6902-3
✔The SAT I For Dummies
0-7645-7193-1
✔Spanish For Dummies
0-7645-5194-9
✔Statistics For Dummies
0-7645-5423-9

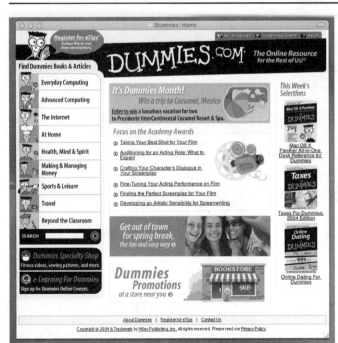

Get smart @ dummies.com®

- **Find a full list of Dummies titles**
- **Look into loads of FREE on-site articles**
- **Sign up for FREE eTips e-mailed to you weekly**
- **See what other products carry the Dummies name**
- **Shop directly from the Dummies bookstore**
- **Enter to win new prizes every month!**